THE ANDREW AND THE ONIONS

The Andrew and The Onions

❦

The Story of the Royal Navy in Bermuda
1795-1975

Lt. Cdr. Ian Stranack, FIL, MBIM,
Royal Navy (Rtd.)

SECOND EDITION

Bermuda Maritime Museum Press
Old Royal Navy Dockyard
BERMUDA

Printed in Canada by
University of Toronto Press

ISBN 0-921560-03-6

The publication of the second edition was made possible
by a generous donation from
Mrs. Thornton Cran
and by funds raised at a dinner held on 16 September, 1988 to
celebrate the 50th Anniversary of the building of The Cottage.

The dinner was given by Commander J.A. Startin, RN and Mrs. Startin
and attended by

Dr. & Mrs. J. Arnell
Mr. & Mrs. J. C. Astwood
Sir James & Lady Astwood
Mr. & Mrs. J. Bluck
Mr. & Mrs. J. Burland
Mr. & Mrs. B. Canty
Mr. & Mrs. H. Cox
Mrs. R. Cox
Mr. & Mrs. W. Cox
Mr. & Mrs. I Fleming
Mr. & Mrs. D. Glynn
Mrs. M. Hamza
Dr. & Mrs. E. Harris
Mr. & Mrs. G. Haycock
Mr. & Mrs. R. Hunnisett
Hon. Mr. Justice & Mrs. Hull
Senator & Mrs. A. Jackson
Mrs. P. Leseur
Mr. & Mrs. S. Ratteray
Mr. & Mrs. R. Shutter
Mr. & Mrs. L. Simmons
Mr. R. Snape
Mr. & Mrs. G. Stanton
Mr. R. Startin
Mr. & Mrs. R. Sturdy
Mr. H. Watlington
Mrs. J. Watlington

CONTENTS

List of Illustrations

Author's Note to First Edition

Most people know that St. Andrew is the Patron Saint of Scotland; many will recall that he is also the protector of sailors, and that for many hundreds of years the Royal Navy has been known by its Seamen as 'The Andrew'.

The term Onion is less well known. In the 19th and 20th centuries the main export from Bermuda consisted of a special type of onion, grown only in these Islands, which became famous for its mild, sweet taste, and which was in no small way responsible for supporting the economy of this tiny island colony.

Of course, in the same way that all Englishmen became known as 'Limeys', as a result of the introduction of lime juice for ships' crews to prevent scurvy during the long ocean voyages, so the name 'Onion' was applied to all Bermudians, and to be known as an Onion is still the proud boast of those fortunate people whose home is so inextricably linked with the Andrew and the Onion.

It is appropriate to add that in order to save confusion, I have throughout used the term Admiralty (or Their Lordships) to refer to what has during the period covered, been called the Navy Board, The Admiralty Board, The Ministry of Defence (Navy), etc.

This book is dedicated to Drew, at whose instance these researches were turned into book form; and to Alistair and Fiona- whose help and forbearance enabled me to visit many parts of the Island, often at inconvenient times, and in preference to more attractive commitments - without whose assistance the task would never have been completed.

Foreword to the First Edition

Bermudians have been fortunate in having so much of their history preserved in the form of Government and Church records and to have had dedicated historians to compile these, such as former Governor Lefroy, Dr. Henry Wilkinson, Mr. W.E.S. Zuill, Sister Jean Kennedy, Mr. W.S. Zuill, Mrs. Terry Tucker and many others over the years.

To these names should now be added Lieutenant-Commander Ian Stranack, for his *The Andrew and The Onions*, described as the story of the Royal Navy in Bermuda.

The settlement of Bermuda began with the wreck of Admiral Sir George Somers on the Islands, and our association with the Royal Navy forms an integral part of our history.

Lieutenant-Commander Stranack's work is one which shows his dedication to the subject matter and is executed with painstaking care, and I commend it to all those interested in the history of these Islands.

Sir Gilbert Cooper, Kt, CBE, ED

Preface to the Second Edition

Lieutenant Commander Ian Stranack was the Resident Naval Officer at HMS *Malabar* towards the end of the 175-year period during which a Royal Navy flag officer flew his broad pennant at Bermuda. Looking out from his office window over the former Royal Naval Dockyard, by then a so-called 'Freeport' of the Bermuda Government, he may well have been prompted to follow the lead of two earlier naval officers and to record the story of the Royal Navy at Bermuda, before it became lost in the course of time.

Having access to Captain Carr's 1893 manuscript history and Lieutenant Brockman's updated version in the 1938 Bermuda *Royal Gazette* as foundation material and having the operational files still existing in his office, Stranack drew on published information available locally to tell the story. By the time he was posted to Turkey in 1974, he had a working draft, which still needed refinement.

Far removed from any further information, Stranack finished the manuscript and transcribed it using an IBM typewriter. He sent the completed history to the Bermuda Island Press and it was published through the support of Sir Gilbert Cooper. With this, for the first time, a history of the Royal Navy at Bermuda appeared in book form.

The book went through several printings after its first appearance in the late 1970s, but has been out-of-print for several years with no plans for a further printing. The Bermuda Maritime Museum Press, recognizing the continuing demand for a popular naval history of Bermuda, obtained the copyright from the author and undertook this revised edition.

The chapters have been reordered, factual errors corrected, and information added where desireable, but the lively flavour of Stranack's original prose has been retained. The Press is indebted to Birgitte Andersen for transferring the text onto a Macintosh computer, to Joyce D. Hall for making revisions and adding many valuable details, to Jill Pollock for proofreading, and to Jane Harris for designing the final volume.

Once again, Bermuda is indebted to an officer of the Royal Navy for recording yet another important part of the Island's history.

Jack Arnell
Bermuda
1989

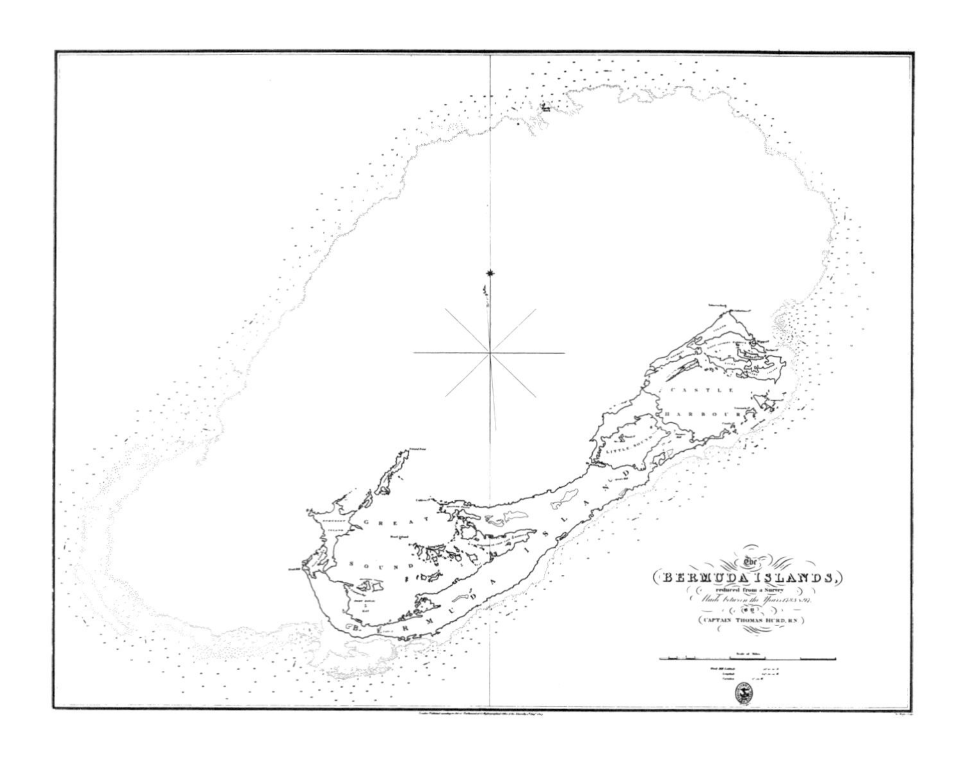

The first published chart of the Bermuda Islands, reduced from the original survey of the area by Captain Thomas Hurd, RN. Published 4th August, 1827. (Hydrographic Office)

The Andrew and The Onions

1

The Development of Bermuda as a Naval Base

Although the Bermudas were discovered little more than a decade after Christopher Columbus' famous voyage of 1492, more than a century was to pass before a permanent settlement was established by the English, following the wreck of the *Sea Venture*, the flagship of a Jamestown, Virginia convoy. There are a number of accounts of visits to the islands in the interim by mariners, who for the most part arrived unexpectedly by way of a shipwreck, and continued their journeys by constructing new vessels out of Bermuda cedar, using items salvaged from their wrecked ships.

From the early days of the colony, Bermudians took to the sea and traded in their locally-built Bermuda cedar vessels to the islands of the Caribbean, the American coast and the fishing grounds of Nova Scotia and Newfoundland. The reefs surrounding the islands were a threat to any unwary mariner, so that Bermuda was shunned by most captains until late in the 18th century. The American Revolution resulted in the end of this conscious avoidance.

With the signing of the Treaty of Paris in 1783, which established the United States of America as an independent nation, Great Britain lost all its naval bases on the North American continent, except Halifax, Nova Scotia. Appreciating this dangerous strategic situation, Sir Guy Carleton, the British Army commander at New York, sent Captain Andrew Durnford of the Royal Engineers to Bermuda to investigate its defence potential. His favorable report led to the arrival of Lieutenant Thomas Hurd of the Royal Navy, a hydrographer, charged with the sounding of existing channels and the search for new ones through the reefs to potential anchorages suitable for the Royal Navy.

Hurd completed his survey of the waters around the east end of the

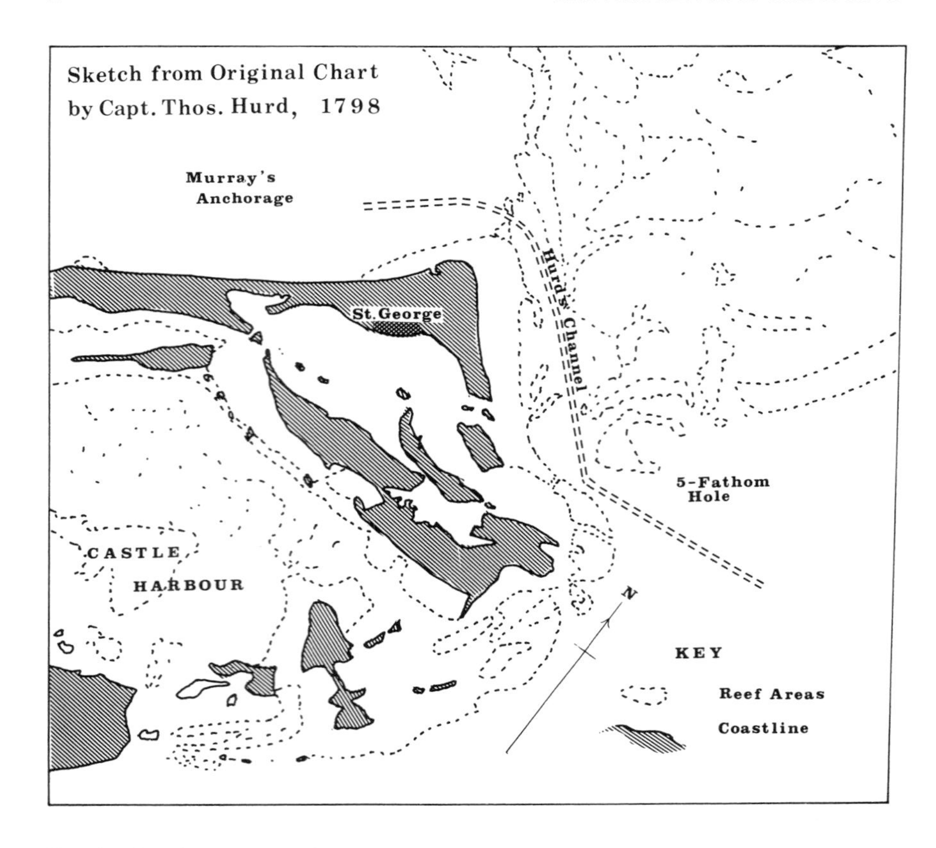

Sketch taken from part of the original Chart of Bermuda, drawn by Captain Thomas Hurd, RN, as a result of his survey, completed in 1791, after some 14 years work. This large, very detailed Chart is labouriously and finely painted to indicate land, shoals and passages through the reefs, and indicates the Channel discovered during this Survey, from Five Fathom Hole to Murray's Anchorage, originally called Hurd's Channel. It was the discovery of this channel, now known as The Narrows, which paved the way for the establishment of the naval base at Ireland Island and which similarly opened up the Port of Hamilton to deep-draught commercial shipping. (From chart at Hydrographic Office)

islands in 1791 and sent his report with charts to the Admiralty in London. This contained the discovery of several channels from the Roads off St. George's (Five Fathom Hole) to a very large anchorage off the north side of St. George's Island, which was to be named Murray's Anchorage a few years later. Hurd continued his surveys, charting the waters to the west of the anchorage as far as Ireland Island, off which he found a second major anchorage, subsequently to be known as Grassy Bay.

The Establishment of a Naval Depot

Following the renewed hostilities between France and Great Britain after the French Revolution, British shipping in the western Atlantic had to be protected against the French Navy and privateers. In May 1794, Rear Admiral George Murray sailed from Plymouth with a naval squadron to reinforce the few frigates stationed at Halifax. Spending the summer cruising off Chesapeake Bay and the Carolinas in search of French vessels, Murray realized that this was a task to be continued through the coming winter and he needed a base to support his patrols during this period.

In early October, Murray learned of Hurd's finding at Bermuda and sent the frigate *Cleopatra* there 'to bring information of a Harbour, which I learned was lately discovered there, fit, it was said, to admit Ships of any Class'. The resulting report described the new anchorage as having 'capacity enough for all the Navies in the World to ride in from 7 to 9 or 10 fm [fathoms]'. Murray was so impressed with the reported potential that he visited Bermuda the following May in the *Resolution*. On his arrival, he anchored in the Roads off St. George's and personally examined 'Hurd's Channel' in a small boat, before ordering his flagship 'to come in whenever the wind permitted which we did with safety the same evening'. Thus he gave his name to the new anchorage.

Bermuda exceeded Murray's expectations as a western Atlantic base for the Royal Navy. Before leaving after his fortnight visit, he named his Flag Captain the 'Superintendent of the Port' at St.George's, directing him to establish a depot there and to purchase several fast Bermuda-built cedar vessels for use as advice boats. At the same time, he proposed that the Admiralty give consideration to creating a permanent shore establishment around the small cove on Ireland Island facing Grassy Bay. The Lords Commissioners of the Admiralty approved the creation of a base at Bermuda, but deferred the plan to use Grassy Bay and Ireland Island until they knew the cost of purchase.

The St. George's depot functioned for some thirteen years, except during the year of peace in 1803, when the squadron was reduced to eight frigates and sloops and the shore staff reduced to a storekeeper and two pilots. With the outbreak of the Napoleonic war in 1804, the shore establishment was reactivated and orders placed for the construction of a large number of small Bermuda cedar vessels.

Royal Dockyard, Ireland Island (1809-1975)

Purchase of Ireland Island

The first official Admiralty interest in Ireland Island appears to have followed the appointment of the Hon. Thomas Grenvill as First Lord of the Admiralty in the autumn of 1806. Faced with the mounting threat from Napoleon and its implications in the western Atlantic, Grenvill resurrected the original proposal of Admiral Murray and sent a letter to the Prime Minister stating that 'the value of (Bermuda) is known to both France and America. Therefore it is desirable that no time should be lost in giving adequate security to it, while it is still ours. ... To secure this great naval station is an object of much national importance.'

Vice Admiral Hon. George Berkeley, the current Commander-in-Chief, did not relish the idea of moving to the uninhabited end of Bermuda, and argued against the proposal until he was succeeded in January 1808 by Vice Admiral Sir John Borlase Warren. Warren immediately surveyed possible sites for the naval yard and sent his report to London in April. This was a balanced document, which considered the potential of Harrington Sound and the large islands of the Great Sound (Ports, Hawkins, Long and Nelly), as well as Ireland Island and St. George's. It confirmed the limited capability of St. George's Harbour to accommodate ships-of-the-line and, while supporting Murray's original concept of using Ireland Island, appeared to favour the islands in the Great Sound.

A year later, Warren was instructed to purchase Ireland Island and to begin construction on it. On 21 October 1809, he reported that

'the Orders for the Establishment of a Dock Yard at Bermuda having been received the Island of Ireland has in consequence therefore been purchased for the Sum £4,800 Sterling in the Great Sound - a Contract has also been entered into for the Wood Work framing of the Storehouse, according to the Navy Board's plan, to be got ready at this place by the end of March next. I request their Lordships will be pleased to direct Captain Hurd to send out, by the speediest conveyance, a Draft upon a large Scale, of the Island of Ireland, of the Cove, Soundings, and point upon which the Wharf should be erected for heaving down a Ship of the Line. It appears to me, that the most secure place would be within the Cove which as it is filled with mud only, may be deepened 15 or 16 feet, the Storehouse built in the Valley, and the Wharf carried out

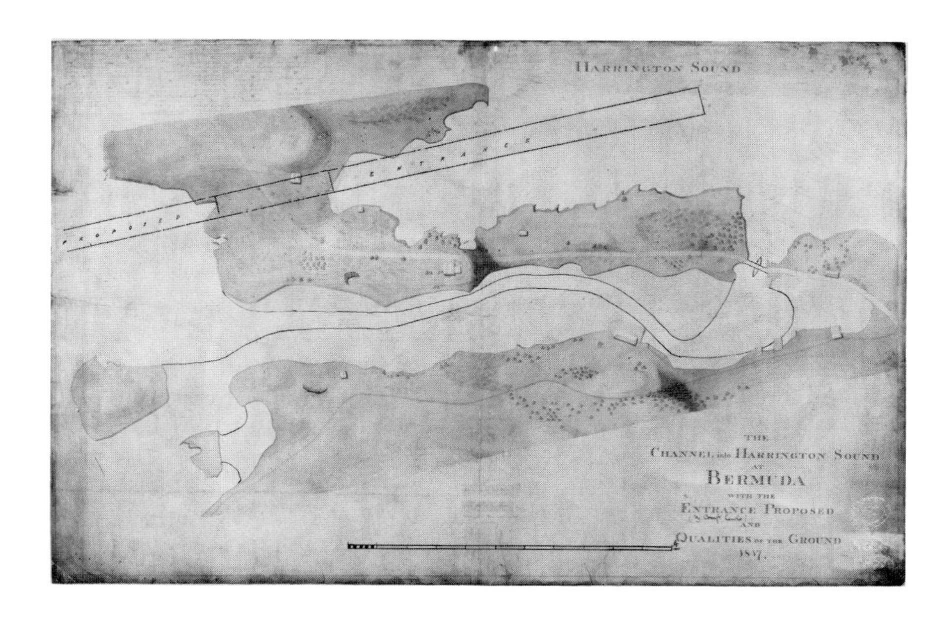

Chart of Flatts Inlet and the entrance to Harrington Sound, 1817, showing the proposed new entrance through Tucker's Bay. This project was abandoned in favour of the Ireland Island site. (Hydrographic Office)

from the North side towards the deepest part of the Center of the Cove, and the Easterly Reef of Rocks to have a pier built upon them which would entirely shelter any ship within the Cove from all points of the Compass'.

At the same time as the main purchase, Warren also bought the islands in the Great Sound, on which he had envisioned a base, paying £828 for Ports, £750 for Hawkins, and £300 for Long and Nelly. These purchases had also been sanctioned by the Legislature in October 1795, when it gave its blessing to Admiral Murray's proposal to use Ireland Island. All the islands had good standing cedar, and steps were taken to prevent the timber being cut before they became Admiralty property. As a result, some 5,500 trees were available to the Navy, and these were bought separately.

The Royal Engineers, who were responsible for constructing the defences for the Dockyard, started by digging ditches and erecting martello towers, with more energy than reason. One of these projects was what was later called Cockburn's Cut, first dug in 1816, but filled in again in 1823. It was reopened in 1843, and a permanent bridge of poured concrete, the first of its kind in Bermuda, was constructed over the Cut in 1892.

The name Ireland Island is thought to have come from that of a Mr. Ireland, who had owned a large part of the area prior to its purchase by the Navy. However, there is a common problem of name-changing in Bermuda, and the origins are often difficult to determine. For instance the part of Ireland Island known as Maria Hill is thought to have derived from Neriah Hill, who owned a house which was at one time nominated as a prospective Admiralty House. Similarly, Boaz Island has, in its time, also been called Gates', Bowes' and Bean's Island.

The Early Buildings

The few buildings which were built in the Dockyard at that time were scattered higgledy-piggledy around Ireland Cove, wherever they could be fitted in. The sketch map by Admiral Warren dated 1811 indicates the original layout. The large storehouse is that depicted in several paintings of that era, with a single tower, which is mentioned variously as having stood until 1842, and eventually as having come down in 1857, when the final three feet of the walls were blasted away to make room for the new storehouse complex as we know it today. The actual date of the final collapse is discussed in a later chapter.

In 1818, a chart was drawn showing a proposed layout of the Naval Dockyard. This shows that the plans for the Dockyard were still very modest, the whole area being surrounded by a small wall with a martello tower and a dry ditch, with a swing-bridge across it, guarding the southerly

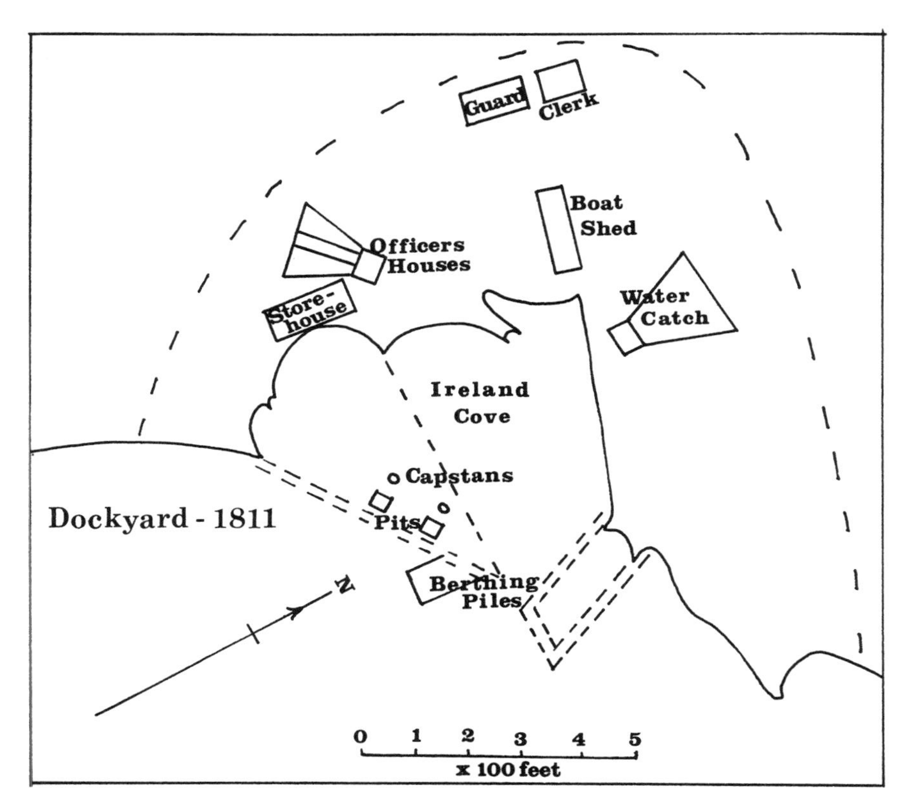

A copy of Vice Admiral Sir, J.B. Warren's sketch-map of the Dockyard, dated 1811, used as part of his handover notes to his successor, Rear Admiral H. Sawyer.

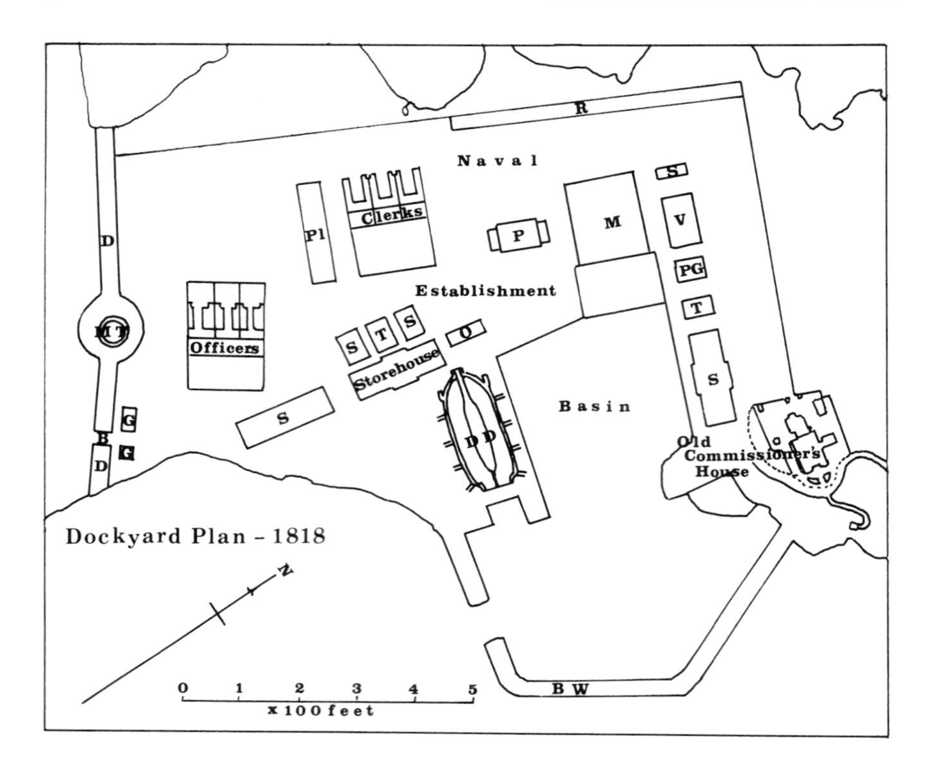

Tracing from Admiralty Chart A.822 by Edward Holl, 30th April, 1818. Buildings in existence in 1818 are named, except the Stores, Tank and Offices adjacent to the Storehouse, which are lettered. All other buildings are those proposed at the time, most of which were never built, or at least not in the positions indicated.

Key

B	*Swing Bridge*	*P*	*Pitch House & Smithery*
BW	*Breakwater*	*PG*	*Paint & Glazier Shop*
D	*Ditch*	*Pl*	*Plank & Timber Store*
DD	*Dry Dock*	*R*	*Rope walk*
G	*Guard House*	*S*	*Storehouses*
M	*Mast andBoat House*	*T*	*Water tanks*
MT	*Martello Tower*	*V*	*Victualling Store*
O	*Offices*		

approach. It is also interesting to see on this chart the modest size of the Superintendent's house at that time, the area being completely undeveloped and wooded, a lone gardener's house occupying the site of the future Commissioner's House (not shown).

However, the construction of the defences was the responsibility of the Army, and these modest plans of the Navy were at once put aside by the Royal Engineers in charge of the works, who obviously found the challenge of the job too much to let it pass as a minor achievement.

By 1812, a boundary had been established and marked using timbers from the hull of the *Ruby*, which was being broken up at the time. In 1826, Captain Fanshawe, Royal Engineers, made a survey of the area, and delineated the Dockyard area from the Casemates* to the Keep. His recommendations were accepted by the Admiralty in preference to those of two other army officers, and in 1827, the Commissioner was exhorted to keep to these boundaries.

The result of the Army's grandiose plans was that, during the period up until 1848, the Navy was unable to lay out their buildings in the manner required, since they were inhibited by the various fortification works and levelling being carried out by the Army. It is relevant here to point out that the area now forming level ground, from the Casemates Barracks to the Keep, was at that time heavily wooded, and rising up to forty-five feet above sea level. The effort involved in levelling this ground by hand can best be left to the imagination.

Thus during this early period, there were virtually no permanent buildings constructed, and the greater part of all ship repair work had to be undertaken at the main dockyard at Halifax, Nova Scotia, or in the Spar Yard.

The Spar Yard, so called because it was originally developed as the fitting yard for masts and spars, was therefore the first area which was occupied by the Navy on Ireland Island. It is situated about one mile to the south of Ireland Cove. The first stone-built building was the guard house, all other sheds in this area being constructed from timber. This area was much used during the early days of the construction of the main Dockyard, and it remained in active use right up until World War I, when a torpedo boat slip and repair shed was in constant use there.

---

* The word 'casemate', for long used in Bermuda when referring to the barracks built at the southern end of the Dockyard, in fact refers to chambers with gun embrasures built into the thickness of the rampart walls. All the walls around the Dockyard are casemated at the corners, where they are built out to provide an angle-of-fire along the adjacent walls.

The War of 1812

The War of 1812 broke out shortly after the new Dockyard was beginning to take shape and before it was able to give more than token support to the expanded North America Squadron. Some measure of the naval activity is found in the 1,593 vessels captured in the West Indies, off the American coast and on the Great Lakes by the Royal Navy and supportive privateers, with Bermudian privateers taking about 300 of them.

One major operation against the Americans was launched from Bermuda. Following the defeat of Napoleon in the spring of 1814, the British were able to devote more attention to the American war and troops no longer needed in the Iberian Peninsula were convoyed to Bermuda for assembly before being sent to the mainland. On arrival in July, they were bivouaced on the level ground along the north shore of Devonshire, where the Navy Wells were located. A contemporary report stated that the assembled warships and transports 'all under the command of Sir Alexander Cochrane in the 80 gun flagship *Tonnant* made as brave a show as Bermuda has ever seen. The fleet at anchor stretched from the Ferry to Spanish Point, all of them in full view of Admiralty House at Mount Wyndham Bailey's Bay'.

Vice Admiral Sir Alexander Cochrane, the Commander-in-Chief, briefed the Navy and Army staff officers on his plan to use this military force in a strong attack on the coast of Maryland or Virginia to relieve the pressure on the British troops around the Great Lakes. After watering, the ships were ready to sail for Chesapeake, but a persistent east wind prevented the heavy warships and the transports from making their way around St. George's Island and through Hurd's Channel to the open ocean. The Admiral had planned to accompany the expedition, but after waiting briefly for the wind to change, he decided to go ahead in the *Tonnant*, accompanied by only the frigate *Surprise*, which was commanded by his son Thomas. They sailed on 1 August.

While it is known for certain that when Rear Admiral Malcolm sailed in the *Royal Oak* two days later with the troops, the wind was still adverse and the ships were piloted out through a dangerous channel beside North Rock on the outer reefs, it appears that the *Tonnant* and *Surprise* were also taken out through this channel, after it had been carefully buoyed by naval officers under the direction of George Renner, the Master Attendant at the Dockyard, who had charge of the King's Pilots. The channel had been similarly buoyed four or five years earlier to permit Vice Admiral Warren to get to sea under the same wind conditions. At that time, Renner had been the master on Warren's flagship *Swiftsure*, so he would have a previous experience with the piloting of a ship-of-the-line through the channel.

This successful feat has been attributed to the piloting skills of at least three different persons by different authors, and probably all three, as well as others, played a part. It must have been a cooperative undertaking involving all with a knowledge of the reef area around North Rock, for conners would have been needed on all the larger vessels.

Once through the reefs, the flotilla had a fair passage to Chesapeake Bay, arriving on 17 August. On entering at ten knots, the *Royal Oak* struck a sand bank, but carried over it without damage and continued up the Bay with the other ships to the mouth of the Patuxent River, where the *Tonnant* and Vice Admiral Cochrane were waiting. Rear Admiral Sir George Cockburn, who had been exploring the surrounding countryside in various disguises, joined the forces as the operational naval commander, with Major General Ross, who had been with the troops in Bermuda, as his army counterpart. The climax of this expedition was the capture of Washington and the burning of the Capitol.

There was an unfortunate incident between USS *President* and HM Frigates *Endymion*, *Pomone* and *Tenedos* on 15 January 1815, just after the peace had been signed. However, because communications were so slow in those days, the ships involved thought that they were still at war. After a running fight of many hours, the *President* was forced to strike her colours. A prize crew was put on board, and brought her to Bermuda, where they first heard that hostilities had ceased.

The *President*, under the command of Commodore Decatur, had fought so well that he had had his sword returned to him, a singular honour to a brave opponent. However, when the ship was brought into St. George's as a prize, it was alleged by some people that the Commodore had ordered part of the ship's crew to hide below decks, with the idea of retaking the vessel. There were various rumors rife at the time, but Lieutenant the Hon. Perceval, of HMS *Tenedos*, who was a member of the prize crew, is stated to have seen these men.

This was considered to be a most deceitful and cunning move, and the Governor considered it impossible that such a brave man as the Commodore could be so unworthy. As a result, the editor of the first *Royal Gazette*, Edward Ward, was dismissed from his post as King's Printer for having dared to publish such a libellous story. In the event, nothing came of the plan, if such it were, and the whole incident simmered down. However, Edward Ward left Bermuda in disgrace, and moved to Canada, where he founded his own newspaper.

A Midshipman, Sutherland Dale, wounded in the engagement, died on 15 February 1815 in St. George's of sepsis of the leg, having been well cared for by the people of the Town. He was buried in St. Peter's graveyard, and a memorial service, symbolic in reaffirming the gratitude of Commodore Richard Dale, Midshipman Dale's father, for the kindness shown to his son by the people of St. George's, for some years was held annually.

Development of the Dockyard

By now the serious business of building the Dockyard was under way. In 1823, the first convict hulk arrived off Ireland Island from England. Until this time, only the following had been employed on the immense task of construction: seventy-four English artificers, fifty-four Bermudian artificers, 164 labourers, and an unspecified number of slaves, hired from their Bermudian owners. In addition, a guard for the convicts, consisting of twenty Royal Marine officers and 393 other ranks, arrived in Bermuda.

To build the Dockyard, large land reclamations were commenced. The Keep and Casemates were built between 1824 and 1842, the main or Great Wharf and the walls of North Yard, between 1827 and 1837.

By 1826, the northeast breakwater was 200 feet long and growing at thirteen feet per month. However, at this stage, there was a severe curtailment in effort on this part of the project and in 1827, only about thirty-five feet were added to the breakwater.

The progress report of 10 September 1829 indicates the slow advance being achieved at that time; cranes and sheerlegs used to lift the heavy blocks from the quarry face were standing idle owing to the lack of convicts to operate them. Only three diving bells were in use, a fourth being awaited from England.

Even so, a plaintive plea for a further six diving bells, 'if the Navy Board thinks it necessary to incur the expense', plus 120 men, conductors, and ten masons to work them, almost certainly fell on deaf ears in England.

The northeast elbow widening was started at this time, but was still incomplete eleven years later. The break at the northeast end of the yard, cut sometime after 1829, was originally to have formed part of a guarded channel to the Keep Yard, where the army arsenal was established, but this was never finished. The now bridged gap left from this project also serves as a means of ensuring that the Dockyard gets washed through during each tide, though the present silting-up of this cut does not make it a very effective cleanser these days. The northeast arm was later used as a coal-heap until proper bunkers were built in 1852.

In 1836, a terrific hurricane hit Bermuda and breached the newly constructed breakwater in three places. Altogether some £30,000 damage was done and several craft and boats were sunk. This storm affected the completion date of the Dockyard considerably, since a great deal of man-power had to be diverted to carrying out repairs, instead of progressing

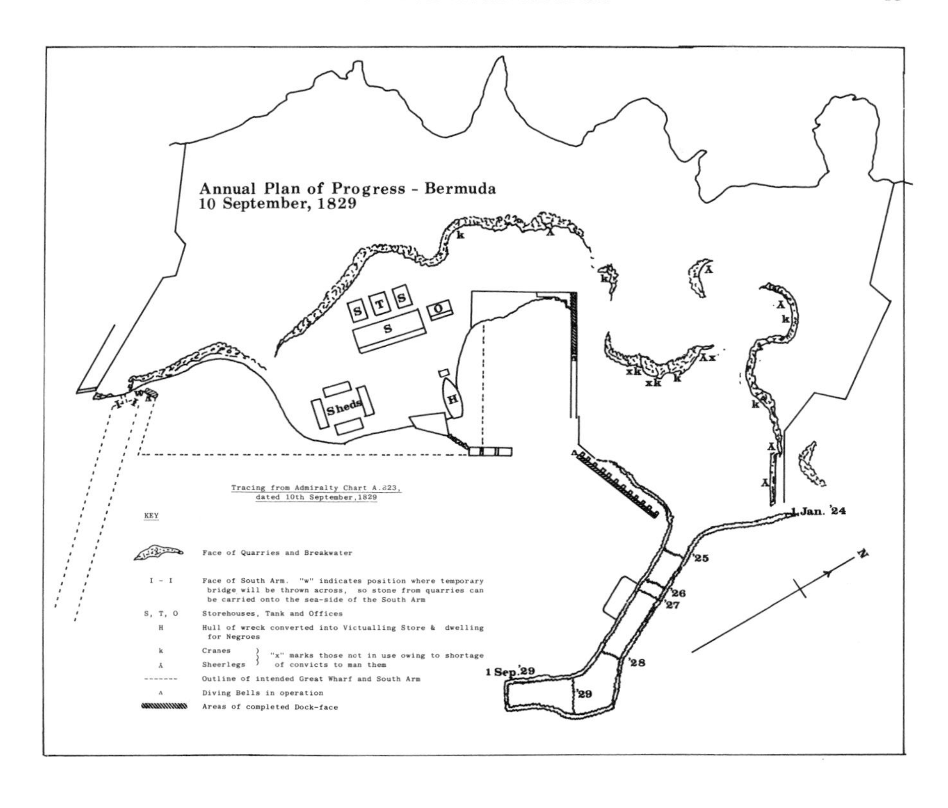
Annual Plan of Progress - Bermuda
10 September, 1829
Sheds
H
S
T
O
1 Jan. '24
'25
'26
'27
'28
'29
1 Sep.'29
N
Tracing from Admiralty Chart A.823,
dated 10th September,1829
KEY
Face of Quarries and Breakwater
I - I
Face of South Arm. "w" indicates position where temporary bridge will be thrown across, so stone from quarries can be carried onto the sea-side of the South Arm
S, T, O
Storehouses, Tank and Offices
H
Hull of wreck converted into Victualling Store & dwelling for Negroes
k
Cranes
Sheerlegs
"x" marks those not in use owing to shortage of convicts to man them
Outline of intended Great Wharf and South Arm
Diving Bells in operation
Areas of completed Dock-face

with new construction.

It was a combination of this delay, the shortage of money, and the political situation at that time which dictated that virtually no work was carried out on the Dockyard between 1837 and 1848, when the energy of Earl Dundonald was directed to ensuring that work was once again resumed on this vast complex.

In 1825, a Mr. Smith had proposed a railway to help with storing. In 1849, it was reported by Captain Denison, Royal Engineers, that railway trucks were to be provided, but on a scale so small our predecessors would have spurned them as useless. Some of the rails can still be seen, but the system was so inadequate as to be a total waste of money.

There were few permanent buildings at this stage, and as late as 1848, when Lord Dundonald took over as Commander-in-Chief, he complained to Admiralty that

'there was nothing in the Yard to defend - the space enclosed by ramparts is an entire void, except the half finished Victualling Store, and 2 small wooden buildings to be pulled down. The space is incapable of holding the Dockyard and Victualling Yard. There is not a Shed in which the Sails of the Flag Ship can be fitted, not even space for setting up a Spunyarn reel out of the rays of the Sun. Water cannot be got for the Ships; the glacis should be plastered and tanks built'.

Whatever the original plan, nothing could have been done until the hill on the northeast side of the cove was excavated.

Although there was no change in the policy regarding the Victualling Yard, perhaps as a result of this letter a smithery was built in 1849, and from then until 1870, coincident with the advent of steam, a great deal of energy was displayed. The Victualling Yard was eventually completed in 1853, and the rest of the Dockyard was largely complete by 1863, when the last of the convicts were removed from Bermuda. At that time, 200 seamen and Royal Marines, mostly the latter, were brought out to man the area.

In the meantime, the largest floating dock in the world was being built at Blackwall, London for use at Bermuda, where the porosity of the local rock precluded the digging of a dry dock. On 28 July 1869, the dock was towed into Grassy Bay, and served well for many years.

Unfortunately, the hurricane of 1878 damaged the dock severely. In the early 1900s it was sold to a German firm, who were so slow in dismantling it that it was towed across to Spanish Point, where it could be broken up at leisure. Its remains can be seen today, since the breaking up was interrupted by World War I, and was never recommenced.

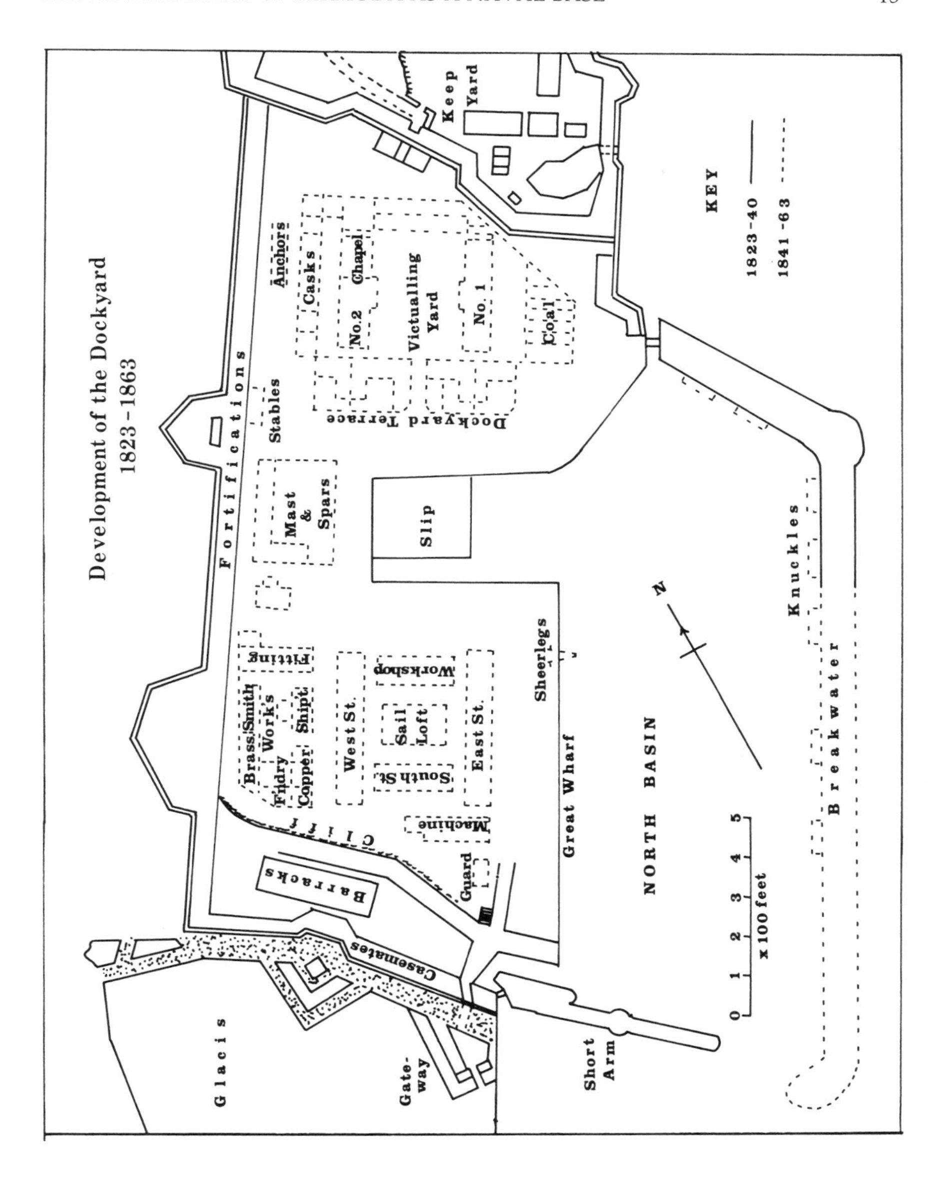
Development of the Dockyard
1823-1863
Fortifications
Keep
Yard
KEY
1823-40
1841-63
Anchors
Casks
Chapel
No.2
Victualling
Yard
No. 1
Coal
Stables
Dockyard Terrace
Mast
&
Spars
Slip
Knuckles
N
Fitting
Workshop
Sheerlegs
Brass Smith
Works
Shipt
Fndry
Copper
West St.
Sail
Loft
East St.
South St.
Machine
Cliff
Great Wharf
NORTH BASIN
Breakwater
Barracks
Guard
0 1 2 3 4 5
x 100 feet
Casemates
Glacis
Gate-
way
Short
Arm

Extension to the Dockyard

The idea of increasing the size of the Dockyard, originally proposed years before by a Mr. Jessop, was brought forward again in 1863. However, approval was not forthcoming on financial grounds, and with the convicts leaving and labour costs increasing, there was at that time no hope of the desired extensions being approved. It is of interest to note that by 1873 the Navy was providing one-sixth of the total income of Bermuda.

In 1897, when Vice Admiral Sir John Fisher, KCB, became Commander-in-Chief, the lethargic approach to naval matters which had prevailed for many years disappeared as if by magic. His boundless energy was directed to making the best use of the facilities available - old ships were ruthlessly scrapped, inefficient officers were sent home, and the Dockyard began once more to bustle with long-unaccustomed activity. The improvements carried out during this period to the defences alone cost some £610,240, which gives an idea of the intense activity created by this dynamic, if controversial, personality.

In 1901, approval was at last given for an extension, almost exactly on the lines proposed by Sir Houston Steward fifty years previously, and in the same year, a contract was let to Messrs. Walker & Co. of London to construct the south arm of the breakwater and an extra 1,800 feet of dockface. At the same time, the defences were modernized for the second time by the installation of guns with the latest rifled barrels.

Construction went ahead apace, and by 1903, a vast quantity of fill had been moved from Moresby Plain to the east shore, and the facings of Portland granite, were in place. The transfer of the fill was carried out largely by a railway system utilising a cut just north of Moresby House, the cut being bridged with a temporary wooden structure, and later refilled when the work was completed.

The task of carving the facings was done by some twenty-five Italian masons, who, with their families, were accomodated in HMS *Terror*, then moored alongside the short arm. They worked well for a while, but later complained about their living conditions, and were replaced and augmented by some 300 Jamaicans, who were accommodated at King's Point in Somerset. They too proved to be unsatisfactory, so the extension works were not fully completed until 1907, though the new yard was in use some two years before.

Building the new wharf involved cutting back towards the roadway along the ridge leading to the North Yard, the fill obtained being pushed into the sea to form a base for the berthing area, and to augment that brought from Moresby Plain. Many houses and other buildings were sacrificed in this project, but the end justified the means, and resulted in a

Ireland Island in 1900, before the building of the South Yard. Note the faint outline of Casemates, the two Dockyard towers, the Sheerlegs, ships in the yard and the floating dock. The ship in the foreground is the Terror, scrapped in 1903. Also in the picture is Moresby Island, with its bowling alley.

Jetty facing stones awaiting placement, 1902 (Godsiff)

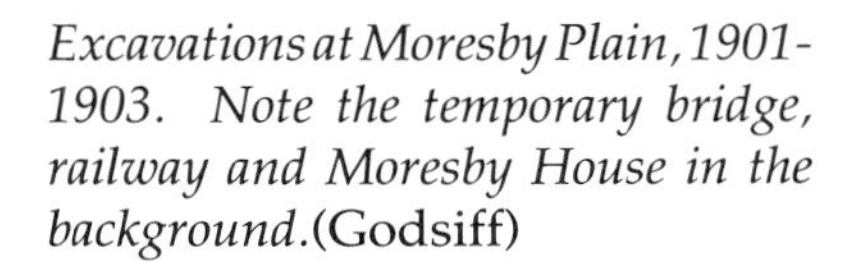

Excavations at Moresby Plain, 1901-1903. Note the temporary bridge, railway and Moresby House in the background.(Godsiff)

very fine berth, with about thirty feet depth of water along its entire length, which has proved its value for berthing all but the largest ships ever since.

The excellence of design and layout of this area is borne out by the fact that virtually no building took place in the Dockyard area after 1907, with the exception of a few temporary buildings, and the resiting of the bollards after the hurricane of October 1926. The total cost of this extension was £700,000.

These developments coincided with the Boer War, when a great many Boer prisoners were sent to Bermuda for accommodation on the islands in the Sound, mainly Long, Ports and Hawkins Islands, all of which were then owned by the Admiralty, under the guardianship of the Army. A total of 4,619 prisoners was kept there during the twelve months that this prisoner-of-war camp was in being, and inevitably some died during their confinement; the cemetary on Long Island bears witness to this. However, it was not until 1903 that it was consecrated and a monument erected to their memory.

During the 1890s, there had been some 1,200 personnel in the Dockyard. As a result of the new programme for the renovation of the defences etc., this number increased to 2,000 by 1904, with twelve or more major warships being present at any one time.

However, by 1907, despite the expense of the new South Yard and the improvements of the defences, the complement was again reduced to 1,000, with a maximum of six ships in harbour together, the new policy of Admiral Fisher, who was by then the First Sea Lord, of Blue Water, rather than Bricks and Mortar - that is, using the strength of the fleet instead of defended shore bases to support Britain's political policies abroad - having been implemented to the full.

On 6 June 1906, a new floating dock, which had been built some four years previously and towed to Bermuda, was moved from the Boss's Cove area into the Dockyard. This vast dock was berthed in the South Yard, on the knuckles built specially for the purpose, and was used during the refitting of many hundreds of ships from then until 1946, when it was found to be too small for the ships then in service. Its replacement, Admiralty Floating Dock No. 5, was in use from 1948 until 1951, when it was towed to England on the closing of the Dockyard.

World War I

With the outbreak of war in 1914, there were five heavy cruisers at Bermuda, including HMS *Monmouth*, the flagship of Rear Admiral Sir Christopher Cradock GFM, KCVO,CB, later sunk in the battle of Coronel, off Chile, with the loss of the Commander-in-Chief.

The war of course brought a considerable increase in naval activity to

Bermuda. However, it was not until the end of 1916, with the enormous increase of sea traffic across the Atlantic carrying food to a beleaguered Europe, that it was necessary to institute an examination service, and a control organization, at Bermuda.

The Examination Service was manned by only one officer, a member of the Royal Naval Reserve, who was transferred from a cruiser which happened to be on the Station at the time. He was responsible for setting up the organization at St. George's, with a bare minimum of facilities, and only two elderly tugs, the *Powerful* and the *Gladisfen*, with which to board and question the master of every vessel which came within ten miles of Bermuda. He was also responsible for taking the pilots to ships wishing to enter Bermuda's ports. During the last two years of the war, this officer boarded and examined the papers of 2,900 ships. It is incongruous that the *Gladisfen* which was built in Germany and owned by the firm founded by W.E. Meyer, a German, was used to such good effect against her place of origin.

Towards the end of 1917, the number of ships of all sorts transiting through Bermuda was further augmented with the entry of the United States into the war, and a great number of extra ships called in both for coal and stores, and also to assemble into convoys to cross the Atlantic under naval escort.

During the war, there were two major hurricanes in Bermuda, one in 1915 and the other in 1916. Both wreaked havoc, one sinking the Commander-in-Chief's yacht, *Pearl*, and the other demolishing Moresby House, the present HMS *Malabar*, which had to be completely rebuilt at a cost of £9,000.

Throughout this period, the personnel serving at the Dockyard were accommodated either in Casemates Barracks, or in the old troopship, HMS *Malabar*, which had been renamed HMS *Terror* in 1901. Although elderly by that time, this ship managed to last through the next eighteen years, before reaching the end of her useful life in 1919. At that time, the Commissioner's House, which had for many years been occupied in turn by the Army and the Royal Marines, reverted to Navy control and became HMS *Malabar*, the home establishment for the Bermuda Dockyard, a task which was carried out from this famous old building until the Dockyard was finally closed in 1951.

In 1919, the Dockyard was again reduced, this time to only 400 personnel, and many of the defensive guns were removed, and sent for scrap, in the vain hope that there would never again be a major world conflict.

During this period the activity in the Dockyard dropped, and in 1929, the yard felt the effects of the world slump, and was reduced to half-strength, in common with many other naval establishments. Even so, those remaining at Bermuda during these years certainly left their mark, particularly on the sporting field, where the rugby and cricket teams of the station cruisers were continually to the fore, beating nearly all local opposition, and even defeating visiting teams from Yale and Harvard Universities.

Luckily the effects of the slump did not last very long and in 1930 and 1932, extensions were built to both the RN Club and Canteen, and the Recreation Club, the Bowling Alley and the Shortwave Radio Station, indicating the continuing interest of the Royal Navy in its base in Bermuda.

Royal Naval Air Station, Bermuda

In 1933, a Royal Air Force Station was established in the Dockyard, a hangar being built on the camber. The station was manned entirely by RAF personnel, and operated first Osprey and later Seafox floatplanes. In 1939, the RAF Station was transferred to the Fleet Air Arm. All of the larger ships serving at Bermuda at that time were fitted with aircraft (Walrus or Seafox) and this additional load was too much for the maintenance facilities available at the camber. A new base, called RN Air Station, Bermuda, with two large hangars, and slipways to the sea on both sides of the island, to allow the aircraft to make best use of calm water, depending on the wind direction, was constructed on Boaz Island.

This air station was active throughout the war, though not in an offensive role, most of the aircraft being used as target tugs for gunfire practice by the warships based at the Island. The station was reduced to care and maintenance in April, 1944.

World War II

Prior to the outbreak of War in 1939, there had been considerable buildup, both of ships and in the activity of the stores and supplies departments. In those days, the Fleet normally went on two cruises each year, visiting ports in South America, the West Indies, North America or Canada. Sometimes individual ships were detached for independent visit programmes, or to assist in relieving natural disasters, hurricanes etc.

On 3 September 1939, the following ships were in Bermuda: HMS *Berwick* (Flagship), HMS *York*, HMS *Orion*, HMS *Ajax*, HMS *Exeter*, HMS *Penzance*, HMS *Dundee*, RFA* *Orangeleaf* (Oiler).

Stores were normally shipped out from the United Kingdom, except for timber and oxygen, which were obtained from Halifax, Nova Scotia. The

---

* RFA means 'Royal Fleet Auxiliary.' The supply ships for the Royal Navy are organized and manned by this service, and not by combatant personnel.

naval activity in Bermuda was intense, with the assembly of convoys and the replenishment and restoring of warships, in addition to the repair work carried out on merchant ships of all Allied Nations, and their naval escorts.

In 1940, Bermuda was established as a Terminal Censorship Base. This meant a great deal of extra mail coming through from ships at sea, all of which had to be read before being forwarded to its destination. Similarly, the communications load increased tremendously, with all signals being in code, and therefore having to be deciphered.

To help with all this extra work, a number of local people were recruited into the Royal Naval Volunteer Reserve. There is no doubt that the hard work and capable manner in which these volunteers carried out their duties enabled the naval authorities to cope with what would otherwise have presented them with an almost insurmountable problem during the early days of the expansion of the base to a wartime footing.

One other activity, manned entirely by Bermudian personnel, was the Examination Service, established, as during the First World War, to check the credentials of all ships entering Bermuda waters. The story of this invaluable service is given in detail in Chapter 12.

Advantage was taken of the deep water training facilities around Bermuda to work up, or prepare for action, ships and their crews after refitting in the United States. Among those worked up during this period were the aircraft carrier *Illustrious*, the battleship *Valiant* and the cruisers *Achilles*, *Perth* and *Emerald*.

Several prize ships were brought to Bermuda after capture, for conversion to the use of the Allies, including *Dusseldorf* (renamed *Poland*), *Hanover* (renamed *Sinbad*), *Lotheringen* (renamed *Empire Salvage*).

One of the most famous ships to come to Bermuda was the armed merchant cruiser, HMS *Jervis Bay*, which sailed from Hamilton early one November day to escort convoy HX 84 across the Atlantic. It was the gallant and selfless action of her captain, Fogarty Fegan VC, and his crew which saved that convoy from the German pocket battleship *Admiral Scheer* on 5 November 1940, and thus enabled a vital convoy to get essential fuel and food to Britain.

It was not all easy going in Bermuda during the war. It must be remembered that everything had to be imported to support both the Base and the local inhabitants. At one particularly difficult time, in 1942, tragedy nearly ensued when the SS *City of Birmingham*, an armed merchantman, which was bringing a large cargo to the Island, was sunk on 29 June. Stocks of cattle and other livestock feed were completely exhausted, and the situation was only just saved by the arrival in the nick of time of another ship with much needed supplies. However, this was not before a comprehensive rationing scheme, covering foodstuffs and animal feed, was introduced. The foodstuffs included butter, lard, sugar, canned milk and soups, and coffee. Tea, however, was not rationed since there was none in the Island at that time. By July, the stock of flour was so low that bread also had to be rationed.

Fortunately by then, the effects of the war were beginning to move away from Bermuda, and it was not very long before a regular store-run was again being made from the United States, by Norwegian Steamer *Braga* , John S. Darrell, agents. This little ship was a lifeline, arriving once every three weeks with 300 tons of cargo. The sole source of frozen foods was by way of U.S. Navy supply ships.

During this rather dismal period, a certain lighthearted interlude met with great amusement in the Island. The quisling propagandist, William Joyce, better known to radio listeners as Lord Haw Haw, decided that morale in Germany needed an added boost, and gravely announced that the forces of the Third Reich had sunk HMS *Malabar*. The only concern in Bermuda was that perhaps the northwest tip of land had fallen off in the night, but a glance from their windows across to Ireland Island confirmed that the Commissioner's House was still there. This particular propaganda was repeated on two further occasions during the War, a tribute both to the longevity of HMS *Malabar* and to the persistance of Lord Haw Haw, if not to his factual accuracy.

In September 1942, all sizes and shapes of landing craft, for use in the North African Invasion operations, staged through Bermuda. A total of 105 Landing Ships (Tank) and 258 Landing Ships (Infantry) passed through the Dockyard, all of which had to be fuelled and stored before sailing on to England.

By 1943, the number of ships working up at Bermuda was so increased that a special section was set up to cope with this important operation. During the following eighteen months, some 160 vessels were worked up, before this facility was closed down in July 1944.

Apart from repairs which were carried out in the Dockyard, several new construction vessels were built in Bermuda, including 4 wooden minesweeping skids, 1 steel water barge, 4 105-feet Fairmile launches and 12 45-foot motor fishing vessels. Several of the fishing vessels can still be seen around the coast, showing that Bermuda's boat builders had not lost their art.

In 1944, the Royal Canadian Navy took over the work up facilities at Convict Bay, St. George's, which was commissioned as HMCS *Somers Isles*, and which remained in commission until August 1945.

By the end of the war, it had been possible to start running down the facilities at the Dockyard, since the flow of ships from the United States to Britain had reduced considerably. With the military cut backs introduced in 1946, it was inevitable that the Dockyard would suffer even further reductions, but it still came as a most unpleasant shock to Bermudians when in 1950 the Admiralty announced that the Dockyard was to be closed within twelve months.

Closure of the Dockyard

Anyone who has had to move house will appreciate the immense task facing those responsible for closing down a complete Dockyard complex. Planning started in early 1950, and was done in the main at the Admiralty in England. The problem consisted of vacating some 360 buildings, shipping some 30,000 tons of stores and equipment, and repatriating some 178 Service personnel, 1,124 civilians and 570 members of their families, as well as dispensing with 2 floating docks and some fifty-eight harbour craft.

The first moves were made at the end of February, with the RFA *Beauharnois* sailing from Bermuda in July on the first of four return voyages. Even after her final journey, there was a vast amount of equipment left, and it was not until 13 July 1951, that *Admiralty Floating Dock No 5* was towed away to England, and the final 800 tons of gear shipped home by commercial freight.

In an operation of this magnitude, it was inevitable that a certain amount of pilfering went on. A great deal of equipment, and a large number of boats were sold, at bargain prices, to local persons. All in all, this tremendous task was accomplished remarkably smoothly, and with commendable efficiency. It was a great pity, however, that more records of the 150 years which the Royal Navy had spent in Bermuda were not left behind for posterity.

The New-Look Naval Base was confined to the Main Wall in the South Yard for berthing of ships, together with a very small building in the old Victualling Yard where the Senior Naval Officer had an office ashore. His main job at that time was a sea-going one, with particular responsibilities in the West Indies.

HMS *Malabar* was paid off at a small ceremony held at the Commissioner's House on 31 March 1951. From then on, the responsibility for all Royal Navy commitments in Bermuda has been vested in the Resident Naval Officer, who initially had his office in one of the houses in Dockyard Terrace and lived in The Cottage.

The Commander-in-Chief, West Indies, continued to maintain his official residence at Admiralty House until 1956, but as most of his time was spent away on the Station, his wife led a fairly quiet and lonely existence there. There were also several other houses, widely separated, which were retained by the Royal Navy for possible future use.

Disposal of Royal Navy Property

As a result of the closure of the Dockyard, the lands vacated by the Royal Navy in Bermuda were offered for sale to the Bermuda Government. On 9 January 1953, the House of Assembly agreed to payment of a sum of £750,000 for all Admiralty property in Bermuda, with the exception of certain buildings, facilities and other properties variously situated around the Island.

It was later found that many of these properties were surplus to naval requirements, and being scattered were thus difficult and costly to manage. They were, moreover, rapidly deteriorating through lack of use and maintenance. A further agreement was therefore drawn up which centralized the naval property around the South Yard berthing area, and on 1 April 1965, the remaining naval property, which included Admiralty House, the houses at Daniel's Head and Prospect, the Parsonage and the two large recreational areas on Boaz Island and in Somerset Village, was all handed over to the Bermuda Government in consideration of a further £165,000 and a compact area of some twenty-seven acres was rented back by the Navy on a 99-year lease for the sum of £10,750 annually.

Certain items were donated by the Royal Navy in memory of the many years of association with Bermuda. These included:

- The Clerks' Cottages of Admiralty House, which were given to the Bermuda Government, and now form part of the Pembroke Youth Club.
- A 1/2-ton Admiralty Pattern Anchor, which was installed on a block of granite at the fork of the road in Mangrove Bay.
- The Silvered Ship's Bell and 4 silver bugles and silver trophies of HMS *Bermuda,* which were given into the safe-keeping of the Bermuda Regiment by the Legislative Council. The bell is now on display at the Bermuda Maritime Museum.

The marble plaques listing the former Commanders-in-Chief of the West Indies Station were removed from Admiralty House at a later date, and were eventually installed, first in the new HMS *Malabar* at Moresby House, and subsequently in the Bermuda Maritime Museum.

Management of the Berthing Area

At first, from 15 March 1951, the Resident Naval Officer, with a very small staff, was the sole representative of the Royal Navy in Bermuda. On 1 June 1965, HMS *Malabar* was recommissioned, this time at Moresby House, which thenceforward became the headquarters of the Senior Naval Officer

Berthing area, HMS Malabar, *showing the Naval area of responsibility (whitened dock face), Moresby House (centre-rear), Prince Alfred Terrace (married quarters) on left, and Gilbert's Green (Senior Rates' Mess) at right centre. Ships in Dockyard, left to right: HNLMS* Amsterdam, *HMS* Sirius, *HMS* Minerva *entering, with HRH the Prince of Wales embarked, 23 February, 1973.* (Official RN photograph)

West Indies 'SNOWI', and a base for the two frigates which were detached to the station from the Fleet in the United Kingdom, each undergoing an assisted maintenance period of up to three weeks duration during the six-month long detachment.

The activity was, however, fairly low for some six years, but a sharp increase in ship visits took place from 1971, when thirty-two ships were berthed, to 1973, when sixty-four ships were handled. This increase was due largely to the withdrawal of the Royal Navy from its bases in the Far East, and the consequent increase in usage of the practice area in the West Indies, but also included a considerable number of ships of foreign and Commonwealth navies.

This of course put quite a strain on the minimal resources at the berthing area, but with the full cooperation and help of the local authorities, and the honorary consuls where appropriate, an efficient and successful liaison was maintained through this busy period.

Unfortunately, this boom in activity was not destined to last, since the 1975 Defence Review ordained that on 1 April 1976, the post of Senior Naval Officer West Indies was to be abolished, and the two frigates withdrawn from the West Indies Station.

However, the post of Resident Naval Officer was retained, upgraded to a commander of the Seaman Specialization, who was supported by some six uniformed personnel and a number of locally employed civilians. The Resident Naval Officer once again moved into The Cottage, and the twenty-seven acres of naval property continue to be rented from the Bermuda Government; so the facility to berth ships will continue for the foreseeable future, though the frequency of these visits is likely to be considerably reduced.

Repercussions of the Closure

The loss of the Dockyard to Bermuda had a far wider effect than just the immediate loss of income to the Island. Over the previous 150 years, it had become the hub around which a great deal of Bermuda's social and sporting life turned, and there was thus a vacuum left in the day-to-day life which took a long time to fill.

The livelihood of 1,000 civilians, mostly living in Somerset, depended entirely on their employment in the Dockyard. Many had been apprenticed in the Yard and learned the skilled trades of plumber, shipwright, mechanic, fitter etc., under expert tuition. The high standard of the present artisans in the Island is due directly to this excellent background, for which no real replacement has yet been found. The apprenctices working in the yard when it closed were taken to English dockyards and housed and paid until their training was completed, when they were returned to Bermuda at Admiralty expense.

The result was a considerable migration from Somerset to Hamilton, where the tourist trade was beginning to boom. This drift towards the city inevitably meant that Somerset, once a thriving metropolis in its own right, became a small underpopulated area, with little to offer the youth of the day, either by way of work or entertainment.

It is sad that 141 acres of lovely Sandys Parish, from Watford Island to Ireland Island, has become a neglected and run down area of Bermuda, but it is confidently hoped that plans to redevelop it for the benefit both of residents and tourists alike will shortly result in a revival of its former glory and healthy activity.

One of the most exciting and promising of these plans is the development of the Dockyard Keep Area as a Maritime Museum, under the auspices of the Bermuda National Trust, designed to make full use of this unique site, both as a museum showing the progress of the many facets of Bermuda's maritime heritage and as a pleasant and intriguing place to visit and marvel at as a reminder of the days when Britain ruled the waves, and left her landmark of magnificent Imperial buildings to bear witness to the great naval achievements of the 18th and 19th centuries.

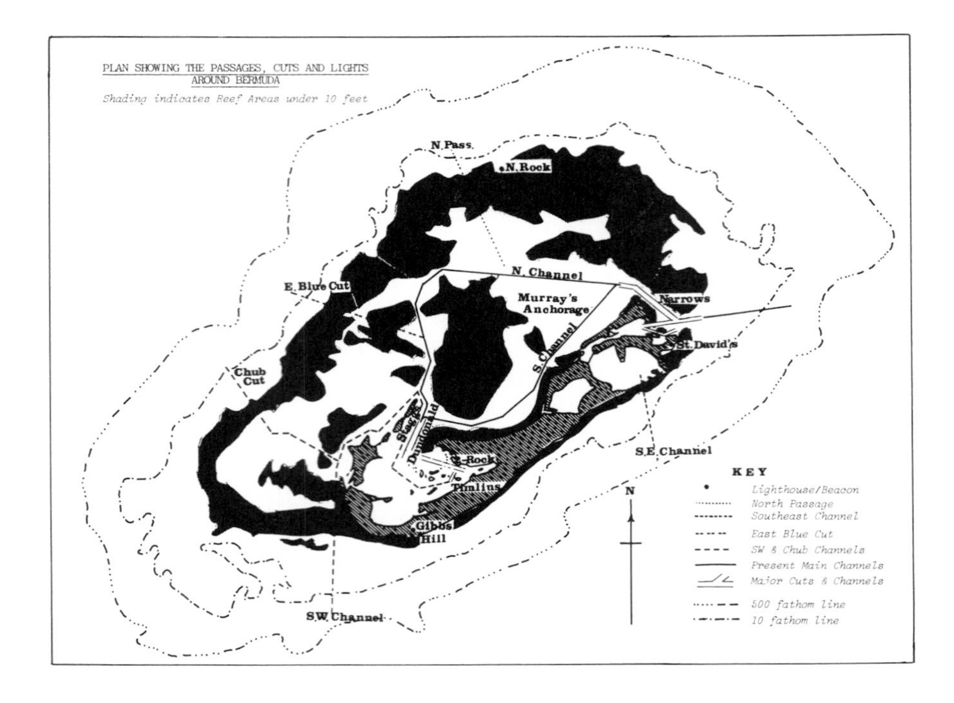
PLAN SHOWING THE PASSAGES, CUTS AND LIGHTS AROUND BERMUDA
Shading indicates Reef Areas under 10 feet
N.Pass.
N.Rock
N.Channel
Murray's Anchorage
Narrows
St.David's
S.Channel
E.Blue Cut
Chub Cut
Dundonald
S.E.Channel
Gibbs Hill
S.W.Channel
N
KEY
Lighthouse/Beacon
North Passage
Southeast Channel
East Blue Cut
SW & Chub Channels
Present Main Channels
Major Cuts & Channels
500 fathom line
10 fathom line

2

Navigational Aids and Approaches

Appointment of Pilots

Thomas Hurd had three slaves helping him with his surveys of Bermuda's waters. These he had trained to be pilots and one of them, James Darrell, brought the *Resolution* into the new anchorage on the day of her arrival in May, 1795. Learning that Darrell was a slave, Admiral Murray wrote to Governor Crauford on the same evening asking that Darrell's freedom be purchased by the Government, so that his 'merit would be rewarded, and others stimulated to qualify themselves for that important Service.' This took a considerable time, but on 1 March, 1796, the Governor signed his release, which read in part:

'A certain Negro Man, commonly called or known by the name of Jemmy Darrell, aged Forty seven years or thereabouts, of a smooth skin and yellowish complexion, and five feet eight inches high, formerly belonging to Mr. Francis Darrell, of the Town of Saint George in these Islands, deceased, and lately purchased by me the representative of the said Francis Darrell: and I do hereby declare the said Jemmy Darrell to be exonerated and released from all and all manner of Slavery or Servitude whatsoever, and I do earnestly request all persons to treat him, as a Man actually and bona fide Free.'

Within a week of his arrival, Murray issued instructions appointing the three slaves - James Darrell, Jacob Pitcar and Tom Bean - to be King's Pilots. They were to be borne on the *Resolution*'s books at the rate of 3d sterling per day and to have their provisions when on board any naval vessel. They were never to be taken away from Bermuda on a departing vessel. Hurd was their supervisor and would direct one of them to board a naval ship approaching the Island and to pilot it to an anchorage. The pilot normally remained on board until the vessel put to sea again. This was in the event of the anchor ropes parting in a gale or other accident which would cause drifting within the anchorage. The value of these pilots was soon recognised within the squadron, and it appears that the freedom of the other two was purchased after Darrell's manumission using squadron funds.

In 1845, Admiral Austin, representing the Admiralty, which was still responsible for the appointments and training of Pilots, revoked the rules for payment of these men, by which they were paid 5s 4d (Warden) and 3s 0d (Pilot) per day, and instituted payment by services rendered. He also ruled that HM Ships could transit to Grassy Bay without using a Pilot, a rule still in effect today.

Lighthouses and Beacons

The purchase of Wreck Hill by the Admiralty in 1795 was undertaken with a view to building a Lighthouse there, to cover the Southwest passage. However, with the usual dilatory approach to these problems, by the time the foundations were eventually laid in 1840, its usefulness was overtaken by the proposal to construct Gibb's Hill Lighthouse, which had far better coverage, and was planned in preference to the Wreck Hill site, since it would cover also the approach along the North Shore to the Dockyard.

Gibb's Hill Lighthouse was completed in May 1846, at a cost of £12,000. It was originally fitted with a rotating paraffin lamp, which was clockwork driven and required winding every half-hour, when the pressure similarly had to be pumped up to the paraffin tank. The lamp was electrified in 1944, and the whole mechanism was replaced with an automatic system in 1951.

A further aid to ships approaching the Island from the East was the construction of the lighthouse at St. David's which first exhibited its light on 3 November, 1879 and still gives clear warning today of the dangerous reefs to vessels as they approach the Narrows. This lighthouse was built with a steady white light, produced by a kerosene vapour burner, which served until 1961 when the light was electrified. In 1965, the entire lighting system at St. David's was electrified.

It was not until 1912, however, that the dangerous North Rock was lit by a beacon, built the previous year by W.B. Smith. This proved somewhat unreliable, but continued in use until 1960, when on August 16th, the new light, equipped with a radar reflector, was installed. More recently, following a number of groundings in the area, a series of beacons have been built on the northern perimeter of the reef.

The Channels

Timlin's Narrows

Since 1836 a proposal had been in abeyance to open up the Port of Hamilton. This was again brought forward in 1840 and it was decided that the passage would best be opened by blasting a rock off Hinson's Island, to open up Timlin's Narrows, a rather circuitous, but otherwise acceptable route to Hamilton via Granaway Deep.

The lowest estimate was £2,700, and three convicts, with the necessary dynamite, boats, etc., were assembled, and work commenced. The problem was a bar of rock, which was some 160 by 160 feet in size and needed to be removed to a depth of seventeen feet.

Work came to an abrupt end on 11 September, when a very fierce hurricane struck the Island with terrific force, causing three large breaches in the Dockyard breakwater. £30,000 worth of damage was done to the Dockyard, and a further £20,000 at St. George's by this storm.

Operations at Timlin's Narrows were suspended for a considerable time since the convicts had to be withdrawn to help with the Dockyard repairs. Three unskilled local men were employed in their place on the rock-blasting, but inevitably there was an accident in which the two men working in the diving bell died. As a result, it was not until eighteen months later (1842) that the project to clear the channel to seventeen feet was completed, at a total cost of £6,415, nearly three times the original estimate.

St. George's

In 1842, work started on the deepening of St. George's Channel, but lack of funds delayed the completion of the full plan to dredge this to eighteen feet and the project dragged on for many years, always taking second place to the other channel projects. A further delay was caused on defence grounds, since the Commander-in-Chief ruled that until the proper heavy guns were installed to cover the approaches, no widening might take place.

In April, 1853, a Select Committee was appointed to investigate the problem of finance in further enlarging this channel. This resulted in a further vote of £30,000 for this project, with the proviso that on completion the dredger-rock cutter would be sold without the expense of a prior refit.

In 1909, the St. George's Channel Act was passed detailing the requirement for opening the Town Cut for shipping. The Government purchased the dredger *Cerne*, but unfortunately she was lost at sea en route for Bermuda from England. Her replacement, the dredger *King George*, commenced work on 24th July, 1911, and on 1 January, 1917, the channel was opened by the Governor, Sir S.G. Bullock, CB, the minimum depth being twenty feet. Further improvements have been made to this channel and the minimum depth in the Town Cut is now maintained at thirty feet.

Staggs and Dundonald Channels and Two Rock Passage

Although small vessels had always been able to pass between the rocks guarding the entrance to Great Sound, the opening up of Hamilton as a major commercial port required the passage of larger ships.

A proposal to enlarge the Staggs Channel had been made in 1836, but had not been progressed, and there was little enthusiasm for expending the estimated £40,000 on this project until a new Colonial Secretary, Captain Archibald Alison arrived in Bermuda. Although a very controversial person politically, he was most active in all matters of dredging, even spending three months at his own expense in St. Lucia and British Guiana to gain from their experience in similar projects.

This scheme included the opening of Two Rock Passage as the main access to Hamilton Harbour, since although Timlin's Narrows had been in use for some fifty years, the tortuous route and the maximum depth of seventeen feet were inadequate for the modern steamers then coming into service.

So the works progressed, with the dredger *Majestic* performing the task with commendable efficiency, and the channel was eventually opened in 1892, at a total cost of £80,000, instead of the original estimate of £40,000. Further widening and dredging took place from time to time after that until the present channel was completed in 1924 to a minimum depth of 30 feet.

In 1915 it was realised that the Staggs Channel had to be enlarged or rerouted, since the larger modern ships then coming to Bermuda could not safely make the turn into the old and narrow Staggs Channel. The recommendation made by the Queen's Harbourmaster, who undertook the study, was that the old Staggs Channel should be abandoned, and that it should be replaced by a new channel, of 150 feet width, dredged to a depth of 28 feet.

By March, 1924, the new channel had been completed some one hundred feet to the east of the Staggs Channel, and was dredged to a minimum depth of twenty five and a half feet. The first ship to use this channel, which was called Dundonald Channel after the Commander-in-Chief of that name, was the SS *Araguaya*, 532 feet in length, with 61 foot beam, 23 1/2 foot draught and a displacement of 10,195 tons, which passed through Two Rock Passage and on into Hamilton on 5 January, 1925. She was the largest ship ever to have reached Hamilton up to that time. The current minimum depth of Two Rock Passage and Dundonald Channel is maintained at thirty feet.

The North Shore Channels

Since the opening of of the Narrows, a channel had been marked close along the North Shore, and ships had been using this for many years despite its shortcomings (lack of buoys, outcrops of shoal, etc.).

In May 1924, £50,000 was made available to the Admiralty towards the cost of widening the channel from the Narrows to Grassy Bay to 450 feet, and to a minimum depth of thirty-four feet. This scheme was not in the event agreed to by the Admiralty, though they did offer to provide a dredger to assist in the operation, and eventually the channel was enlarged to 300 feet and to a depth of thirty-one feet by March 1926. Minor alterations were also carried out to the buoyage to improve the straightness of the channel, and cover certain shoals.

In due course, a deeper channel, known as the North Channel, was buoyed around the North of Murray's Anchorage, using the same route to connect with Dundonald Channel as had been used for the North and East Channels of the early days. This channel is now used for all ships drawing over twenty-eight feet.

In 1928, the Channel Authority was taken over by the Board of Trade, who also took over the responsibility for pilots from the Admiralty. These duties were taken over by the Bermuda Government, Marine and Ports Department in 1961.

Position and Time Zone

The exact position of Commissioner's House is noted on a stone let into the wall at the front of the building which reads:

Latitude 32 19' 45" North
Longitude 64 51' 25" West
Observed by Captain Jas. Scott
HMS President
Confirmed by Rd. Owen Esq.
HMS Thunder
Commodore Sir Thos. Ussher CB KCH (sic)
Superintendent HM Naval Yard
1836

In a letter dated 7 May, 1898, the Commander-in-Chief informed the Governor that the difference of time from the Standard Meridian of Greenwich and the Clock Tower in Dockyard is 4 hours 19 minutes and 18.3 seconds. A stone giving these figures is let into the base of the Tide Gauge

Tower. This was incorporated in Bermuda laws on 8 November, 1929, as being four hours aheadof Greenwich, now known as Time Zone Q for navigational purposes.

Note: It may explain why Bermuda remained for many years so little known, and thus feared as a "phantom Island" when as late as 1694 it position was given as Lat. 32 15N, Long. 61.10W, some 3 degrees East of it actual positions.

3

The Dockyard Defences

The discovery of the Narrows (Hurd's Channel) has already been covered in Chapter 1, but the importance of this channel as a major part of the defensive aspect of Bermuda cannot be over emphasized.

The Narrows are some one and a half miles long, and even today are only 200 feet wide. At the outer end, near Five Fathom Hole, there is a sharp bend to be negotiated which ensures ships can only pass at a very slow speed, and which of course presented a severe obstacle to square-rigged sailing ships.

Added to this, the construction of Fort St. Catherine guarding the northern end of the Narrows meant that the channel was covered more than adequately by a strong battery of guns. An enemy ship attempting to enter the passage would be almost certain of destruction before it had a chance to bring a major broadside to bear on the fort, since the narrowness and direction of the channel gave no latitude for manoeuvre.

Thus, whilst opening the way to the development of Bermuda commercially, the Narrows effectively screened the Island from any attempt at aggression; and of course, such was this deterrent that Bermuda never suffered enemy attack.

Defence Plan, 1861

However, while appreciating the natural advantages of Bermuda's position, the Commander-in-Chief did take sensible precautions by way of defence plans, the details of one of which are given below.

The reason for the heavy defences was to defend the Dockyard from the continual threat from the Americans during the War of 1812, as well as the threats at various times from Napoleon's forces in the West Indies, and later on, from the Fenians.

The massive defences included forts at strategic points all around the coast, particularly at St. Catherine's Point, Scaur Hill in Somerset and on Paget Island, off St. George's Channel, where the fabulous Fort Cunningham, said to be one of the most strongly-built fortresses in the world, and the only one in the western hemisphere to be constructed with nickel-steel lined redoubts, was eventually constructed! It took eight years to build, being completed in 1845.

However, in 1840, Governor Reid, a Royal Engineer, found the defences totally inadequate and instigated the greater part of the defence scheme. Liaison between the Army, which was responsible for the construction and manning of the Garrison, and the defence of the naval installations, and the Navy was, on the whole, very good, and by 1842 there were 159 artillery pieces protecting the North Shore alone! In addition, the forts around St. George's were modernised and armed, as was Fort Hamilton.

In 1862, the Commander-in-Chief wrote to Colonel Munro, who was in command of the army forces in Bermuda, forwarding the plans for the defence of Bermuda in the event of a sudden surprise attack. This read as follows:

Nile at Bermuda
28th of December, 1861
Memorandum of the contemplated Naval Measures for the defence of Bermuda

1. An Attack on Ireland Island and Somerset

This might be attempted through the Chub Cut, or other of the small Western Entrances; In such a case the two Gun Boats, the *Kite* and Launches of H.M. Ships would be ready to act in shallow water; HM ship *Terror* and other vessels drawing less than 18 feet of water would go round the west of Ireland, pass up to Somerset, and defend the outer Entrances, or be prepared to act as Circumstances might require.

2. An Attack on St. George's

I consider any such attack ought to be successfully resisted by the Batteries at St. George's, but in the event of its being confined to the E. end alone HM Ships in Harbour would be ordered to assume a position to rake the Narrows and prevent the entry of ships.

3. Entry of an Enemy's Squadron by the North Rock

These entrances must be defended by the Navy alone and such vessels as may be at the disposal of the Senior Naval Officer.

4. An Attack and an Attempt to land on the South side of the Main Island

In this case HM Ships, if any in Harbour, and if of sufficient force, would proceed outside to resist any Naval Squadron; the Gunboats and Ships Launches and Boats would act in the great sound wherever it might be found necessary, and any ships drawing less than 17 feet of water would also enter the Great Sound for the defence of Hamilton, Somerset Bridge, etc.; I would also be prepared to land Field Pieces with a body of Seamen and Marines of the Squadron to aid the Military Force, but I think the Military Authorities should establish heavy guns on Field Carriages and keep them in Hamilton for the Special defence of this coast. (Note: The Naval Brigade in India had HMS *Shannon's* 68 Pr. of 65(?) mounted on Field Carriages and they were employed during the Campaign. (Sgd. A. Milne).

5. A combined attack on St. George's and the landing of Troops on the South Coast
   In such an emergency, St. George's must defend its own position, and the Military Force might look for assistance and support as explained in No. 4, and an Enemy forming a lodgement in Somerset ought to be driven out by the Guns of the Ships and the mortars from Ireland.
6. With reference to the S W Entrance, by the Hog Fish Cut, I am of opinion some shore defence ought to be established to protect the entrance.
7. Castle Harbour is at present open to the entry of Steam Vessels. I would endeavour to attack any ships seeking refuge in Castle Harbour from the outside by the Ships of the Squadron and by Gun boats and Ships Launches, from between Long Bend and St. David's Island, but this can only be considered a secondary measure, the Military Authorities ought in my opinion to place mortars and heavy guns in such positions as to destroy any Enemy ships entering that Harbour.
8. Should War be declared I would be prepared to recommend and carry out the following measures:

a. To request the Government to issue a Proclamation making it illegal for any Pilot to bring a ship into Bermuda except through the Narrows at St. George's.
b. The removal of the Buoys at the Narrows
c. That the Dockyard artificers should be stationed to the heavy guns; also if considered advisable, the extinguishing of the light on Gibb's Hill on the appearance knowledge of an Enemy's Squadron being at sea

9. In the defence of Bermuda it is my decided opinion that the Ships of the Squadron intended for the purposes of Blockade, or to protect the extensive Commerce of Great Britain, ought not to be in any manner considered as necessary, or be detained in Harbour for Island defence; The Island's Forts and Garrison with the *Terror* and 2 Gun boats must alone be looked upon for this purpose, and the Admiral in Command could only detain effective Seagoing ships in Harbour, and divest them from other service, from the conviction of the Island being open to attack or capture by the weakness of its Garrison, or of its Military defence.

(Sgd.) A. Milne
Vice Admiral & Commander in Chief

In 1882, the Governor, Lieutenant General T. L. G. Galloway, recognised a danger from the Fenians, an Irish-American revolutionary sect, and on inspecting the defences found them weaker than they had been a decade earlier! Ammunition dumps were 'merely covered from the rain by the equivalent of the most delicate Sevres Vases'. Only two guns were installed at Dockyard, one 4-inch and one 5-inch, plus the gunboats *Scorpion, Vixen* and *Viper,* whose useful life was at an end, but which were available for scuttling to protect the Channel. *Vixen* was, in fact, scuttled in the Southwest Channel off Daniel's Head, though not very effectively, and can still be seen. She forms a haunt for many lovely fish and is a great attraction for 'bottom-peeping' tourists.

The only means of communication, military and civilian, outside the Island was by ship. There was a regular despatch boat which plied to and from Halifax, the nearest main naval base, each fortnight. The journey normally took about two days and three hours. One such journey was completed in good time from Halifax to St. George's, but on transiting the Narrows the wind fell, and it took the despatch boat a further two and a half days to reach Ireland Island! Doubtless a boat was sent to collect the despatches, but anyone who has been becalmed along North Shore will feel sympathetic towards the captain and crew during their frustrating wait for a breeze.

It was therefore with a sense of considerable relief, as well as one of achievement, when the first cable was laid from Halifax, and brought into use on 10 July 1890 with a message by the Governor Lieutenant General Sir Edward Nedigate-Nedegate to Her Majesty Queen Victoria.

The total cost of the military works in the Dockyard from 1830-1945 was of the order of £1,500,000, together with the lives of some 2,500 convicts!

The Keep

The Keep, or Inner Yard, is perhaps one of the most fascinating places in the whole Dockyard area, though, as it happens, it did not come under the direct control of the Navy until after 1930.

It was constructed around a natural pool, fed through a cleft in the cliffs, which was cleverly turned into an almost impregnable magazine area by the army engineers, and in fact contains three of the earliest permanent buildings in the Dockyard. It is of particular interest that the buildings around the pool are the only ones in the entire Dockyard to carry the date of the construction, with the exception of a small door to the outer wall of the Victualling Yard.

The first buildings, constructed in 1837, are of comparatively simple design. They have bricked, arched ceilings, and wooden floors. These were supplemented by the further buildings, constructed in 1849, 1850 and 1852 respectively, which were built in the same style as the remainder of the Dockyard. The one built in 1850 has an example of the most perfect brickwork arching, with the raised pointing between the bricks remaining in excellent condition. This gives an effect almost like that of a church vault. However, the special composite-covered floor, originally lined with lead, indicates only too plainly that the building was used for the stowage of munitions, rather than for more peaceful purpose. It is a pity that the travelling gantry-crane, installed in 1918, rather spoils the effect of this superb ceiling, but such is progress!

The remaining building of the planned complex, the Gun Wharf Store, reflects an unusual history. Although it was designed to be compatible with the 1850 and 1852 buildings, being intended for workshops and offices, it was to have doors opening on to balconies along the front of the second storey. Construction started in 1853, but was halted later that year or early in the next. Late in the summer of 1853, the Dockyard experienced one of its periodic epidemics of yellow fever, during which 138 men were hospitalized, of whom thirty-eight died, and probably many others were taken sick. This undoubtedly interferred with the construction, and, if it did not stop it entirely, the outbreak of the Crimean War the following March did. The building stood for 30-40 years with its lower walls complete and with two-third of the second storey floor of Yorkshire paving stones set in cast iron beams in place. Late in the 19th century, the second storey was added. This was built in the conventional style of the day with a single course of Bermuda stone held together with mortar, in contrast to the three-foot thick fitted stone walls of the lower storey, and a wooden truss roof.

Contemporary charts show lines around Commissioner's Point and entrance to the Keep Pond indicating the line to which large rocks were placed to prevent assault on the walls of the fortifications by small boats; the idea being that the crew of an approaching boat would have to disembark well clear of the walls, and would therefore be in full view of the defenders. The line of these rocks is still clearly visible, and is shown on the plan of the Keep Yard on page 40.

There is a cavernous passageway from the southeast corner of the Keep Yard, which was cut through solid rock in order to give direct access from the ammunition storehouses to the Dockyard. This tunnel, which may be partly natural, was blocked off at the Dockyard end, presumably in 1892 when the coal bunkers were constructed. There are unusually shaped buttresses to the outer wall of the Dockyard at this point which, together with the evidence of the contemporary plans of the area, indicate that there

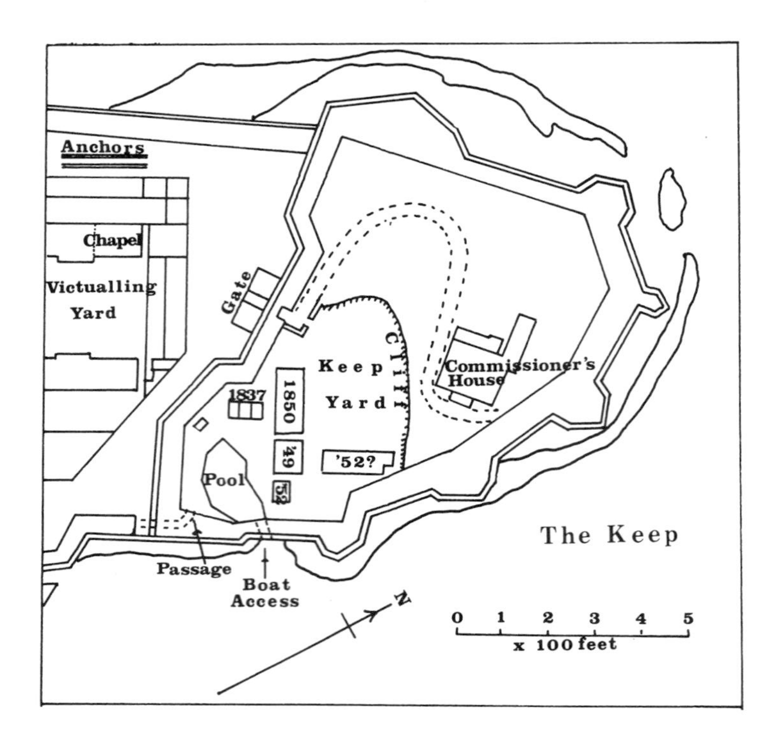

Plan of the Keep Yard. Access to this area, which was under the control of the Army, was through the gate which was fitted with a drawbridge over a tidal moat. A portcullis guarded the boat access. The passage marked on the sketch leads into a caponier, and out into the Dockyard.

The Keep Yard, showing the Keep Pond and ammunition shifting houses in 1974, now restored as the exhibition halls of the Bermuda Maritime Museum.

was at one time a covered passageway to this entrance from the jetty.

Control of the Keep magazine was retained by the Army until 1930, when the installation was taken over as the RN Ordnance Depot, and it remained under naval control until the Dockyard closed in 1951.

Naval watering tanks, Tobacco Bay. From an engraving, 1809.

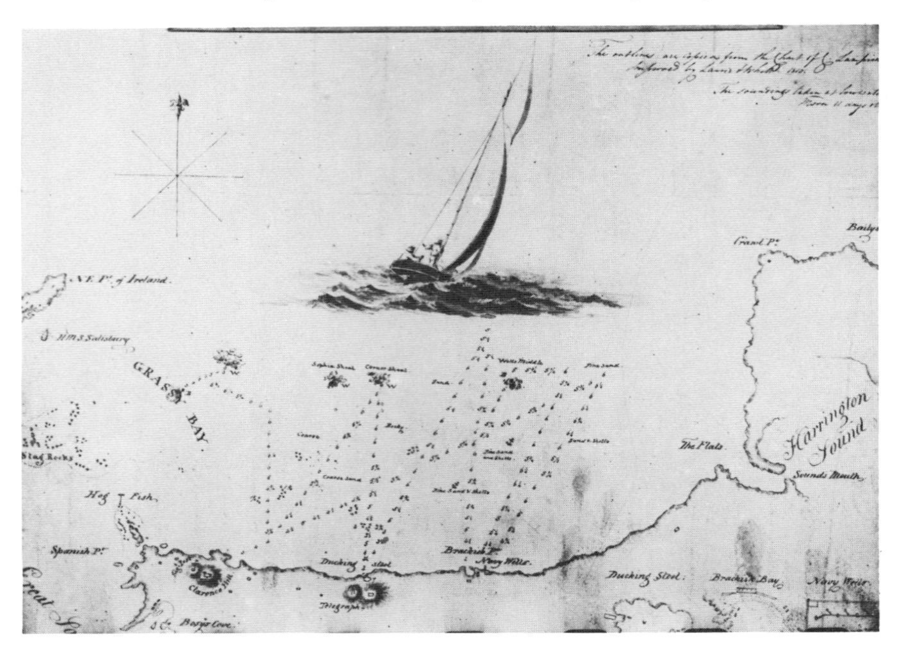

North Shore, 1810, showing the Navy Wells near Devonshire Dock.

4

Dockyard Facilities

Water

One of the big problems in Bermuda has always been an adequate supply of water. The Navy of course had to supply water to the ships, and since there is no natural source of water in the Islands and distillation in large quantities was in those days unheard-of, the first project on setting up a base in the Island was to build a catchment and tanks for this purpose.

The Naval Watering Tanks were established at Tobacco Bay on St. George's Island at Admiral Murray's request of 1795, funds having been voted for the purpose by the Bermuda Legislature. The first ship to make use of the facilities was the *Hermione,* which later had the rather dubious distinction of suffering the worst mutiny in the history of the Royal Navy.

Because the Naval Tanks were not built immediately, a second watering facility was purchased from a Mr. Robinson in 1795 at an area in Brackish Pond (Devonshire), along the North Shore. This consisted of seven wells, known as the 'Navy Wells'. They lived up to the descriptive name of the site, and were in use until 1848, when they were, to the delight of the sailors who had suffered from their tainted water, officially pronounced 'bad' by Lord Dundonald, who had them closed.

The St. George's tanks were used until 1866, when they were handed over to the Army, as the Navy had established water tanks at Ireland Island by that time, but the Navy still retained the right to use the tanks when necessary.

When the Dockyard was developed in later years, many of the bastions were turned into most effective catchments. Extra water tanks were built right up until 1940, and these, together with those already in existence have

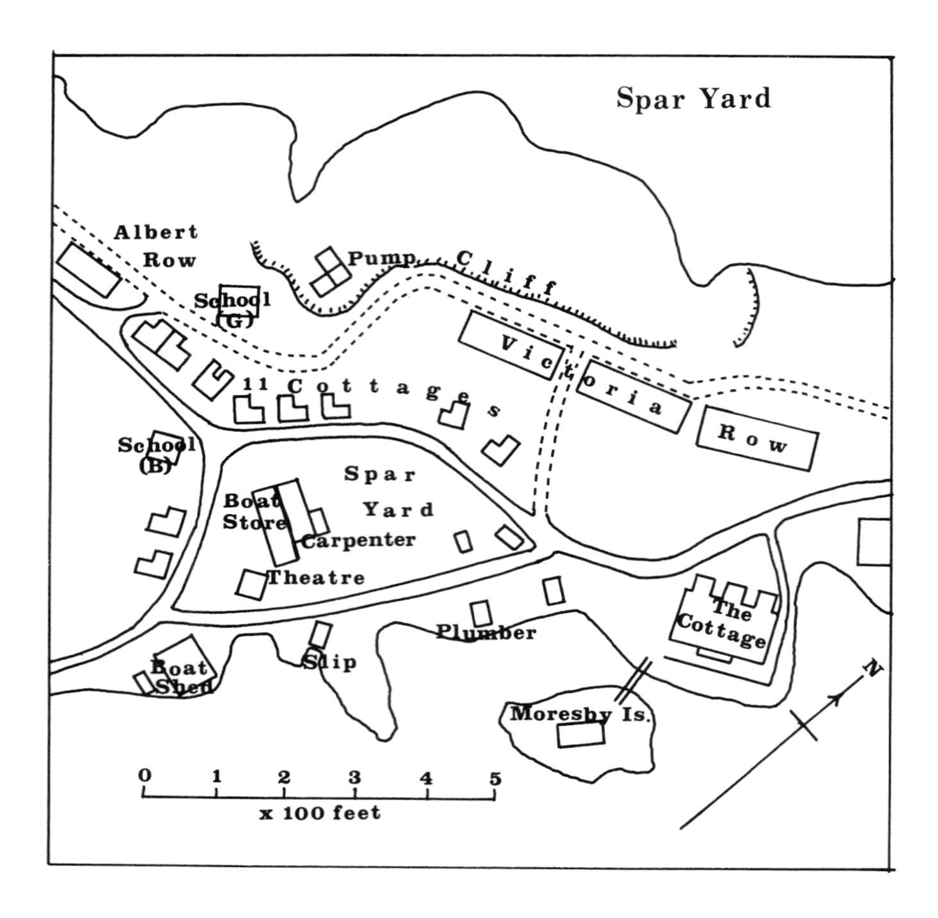

Plan of the Spar Yard circa 1881. This was the first area to be occupied by the Navy (in 1814), since the work on the fortifications did not allow the development of the Dockyard until the 1850s.

a capacity of about 19,000 tons of water. 35,000 tons per year are still available free of charge to the Royal Navy, the remainder being used by the West End Development Corporation.

The Spar Yard

Although it played a great part in the early development of the Dockyard, this area is long forgotten as one of great activity. Its claim to fame is that it was the first area where the Royal Navy set up shore facilities on Ireland Island in 1809. By December of that year, a stone-built guard house had been erected, as well as several wooden sheds. The whole area measured only 500 x 300 feet.

In 1814, a blacksmith's shop was built, and about this time spar and timber sheds were built on ground which had been cut and levelled at the head of this (then) sandy bay. In 1840, ten cottages were erected in the Spar Yard area for the families of Dockyard employees working there. The Boat Store was constructed in 1845.

During the hurricane of 1843, all these wooden buildings had their roofs blown off, but they were repaired and continued in use until 1867. A small slip, cut in the rock below the south gate to the Spar Yard, was made specially to take the schooner *Pickle* in 1847. It was during Captain Aplin's time as Captain-in-Charge, (1871-76) that the blacksmith's shop was converted into a theatre for amateur dramatics, performed by the Dockyard staff, naval personnel and their families. This enterprising project was financed largely from profits made by the Ginger Beer Factory.

In 1893-94, a torpedo boat slipway and repair shed was built at the Spar Yard. It was the construction of the foundations of this slipway which ruined the sandy bottom of the bay. It was designed with a marine-railway slip so that the steam-driven torpedo boats could be hauled out of the water, turned 90° on a turntable, and wheeled into the shed for maintenance out of the weather - a concept of repair work under cover which has only recently been revived as a result of a very long and complex work study on the refitting of submarines and small ships!

With the building up of the main Dockyard, and the arrival of deep-draught, steel-hulled and steam-driven warships, the use of the Spar Yard declined, and apart from being used as a small boat slip, it was not much frequented in more modern times. Although used for some time as a private boatyard and repair shop, the site is now abandoned, and very overgrown. The cottages nearby, however remain occupied, and no doubt the yard, with its enormous slipways will find new life in the not too distant future.

The Main Dockyard Buildings

Storehouses
It is unfortunate that many old records of the Dockyard were needlessly destroyed by an over-zealous clerical staff before 1894. The task of research in this area is therefore considerably hampered.

However, it is certain that there were few permanent buildings constructed within the Dockyard area, which was surrounded by the main fortifications, until after 1848, when Earl Dundonald brought his energy to bear on the problem. The casemates in the south wall were the first to be built (1824) and the building in the Keep Yard dated 1837 was probably the next, but apart from these, the only structures in existence when Lord Dundonald wrote to the Admiralty in 1848 were what he considered to be temporary except, of course, for the Commissioner's House.

Up to now, the only authority on the Dockyard, since Captain Carr wrote his manuscript in 1893, has been Lieutenant Brockman (1932), who stated that the roof of the Great Storehouse, built in 1810, was too heavy and collapsed in 1823, the building being reconstructed with two towers in that year, being what is well known today as the 'Clock-tower Building', officially called the East Storehouse.

However, careful research into this matter, which did not 'fit' into the known development plan of the Dockyard, has proved conclusively that these two storehouses have no common basis at all. This is borne out in several ways; firstly, the handover notes of Admiral Warren to his successor, Rear Admiral Sawyer, which included a sketch, dated 1811, of the plan of the Dockyard at that time, with the position of the old storehouse shown.

This sketch is supported by Admiralty Charts of that era*, which agree exactly on the position of the old storehouse, well set back from what is now the Great Wharf, where the East Storehouse is situated on reclaimed ground. This is, moreover, fully confirmed by the recently discovered Le Marchant paintings (ca. 1857), which clearly show the two storehouses in being at the same time.

The chart of the area as surveyed by HMS *Thunder* in 1843-45 also shows the old storehouse. One copy of this chart has been amended and superscribed, in about 1856-57, by a J. Parsons of HMS *Scorpion*, to show the 'new' Dockyard complex, and this drawing also shows the old storehouse in its position near the Sail Loft and Workshop Buildings, and set at an angle to the new block then being constructed.

However, the mystery is further clouded by Admiralty Chart A 1801

* Admiralty Charts A 822 dated 30 April, 1818, and A 823 dated 10 September, 1829

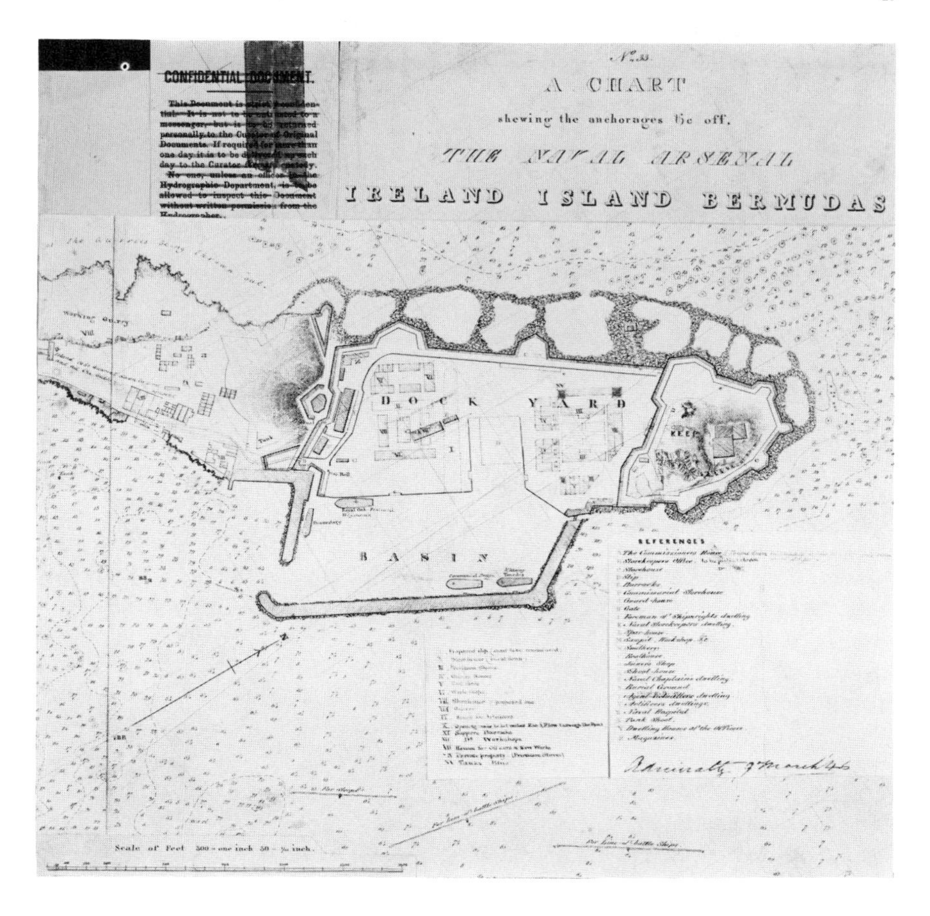

Part of the Chart of Survey by HMS Thunder, *1843-1845, with additions showing the proposed plan of the 'new' yard, superscribed by J. Parsons, RN, during the period 1854-1857. This shows a great deal of detail, including the Keep, Commissioner's House, Casemates Barracks, and also the old Storehouse in its position near the Camber, and at an angle to the present complex of buildings. This Chart was being used for planning purposes in connection with the extensions to the Dockyard in 1857-60, and provides confirmation of the separate existence of the two towered buildings.* (Hydrographic Office)

The old Storehouse, built in 1810, was the first major structure in the Dockyard. It was demolished about 1857, when the new Storehouse complex was under construction.

The East Storehouse, known today as the Clocktower building, has been a Dockyard landmark since its completion in 1857.

The Victualling Yard (east side), 1974.

dated 20 May 1856, which shows the Sail Loft, and Eastern Storehouse as completed, while the Workshops and Western Storehouse are shown dotted-in and marked 'not completed'. The old storehouse is not shown on this plan, presumably since it had by then been at least partly demolished to make way for the Sail Loft. This theory is supported by the fact that the workshop had not been completed, and it is that building which now stands on the ground originally covered by the old storehouse, the demolition of which probably delayed the building of the new structure.

It is thus conclusively proved that the old storehouse, far from collapsing in 1823, lasted for a further thirty-five years or so before being demolished to make way for the new storehouse complex. The final date of demise of the old storehouse is still not exactly certain, but records exist to say it was finally burnt down, apparently prior to May 1856, since the Sail Loft had been built over part of the same site by that time.

The East Storehouse, therefore is not one of the oldest buildings in the Dockyard, as has long been assumed, but was in fact built about 1856. However, in view of its most impressive appearance, it is worthy of a more detailed description.

Of the twin-towers, each 101 feet in height, the southernmost contained the clock, a fine timepiece constructed in Clerkenwell, England, by John Moore and Sons, in 1856. The original mechanism, which had fallen into disrepair after the closing of the Dockyard, was moved to the Maritime Museum, and is now on display, fully restored to working order. It has been replaced, in the tower, by a modern quartz mechanism, which does not require daily winding and attention.

The northerly tower is the bell tower, which contained a bell inscribed 'Evelyn - Haste When I Call' and 'Captain T. Barnardiston, RN, Bermuda, August, 1883'. It was used daily from 1883 until the Dockyard closed in 1951, to summon the workmen, and is now on display at the Maritime Museum. This tower also has a tide-indicator, referred to locally as the tide-gauge, indicated the state of the tide to ships entering and leaving harbour.

One of the other buildings in this complex is of particular interest - the Western Storehouse. This was completed by about 1854-55, but was set on fire by a disgruntled convict, and so had to be rebuilt. No doubt the other convicts who had sweated over this building for several years were not over-pleased with their fellow prisoner! One imagines his 'unofficial' punishment to have been far worse than that meted out by the authorities!

The Sail Loft

The Sail Loft is perhaps one of the most impressive buildings (c.1855-56), from the inside at least, being constructed as it is on top of a huge water tank. Its floor is of teak planks, designed not to damage with splinters the canvas of ships' main sails when being repaired or cut. It is unfortunate that this long-awaited loft was not constructed until steam had already begun to force the sailing ship into the background. However, good use was made of the loft, both as a dance hall and, before and during the Second World War, as a cinema and a theatre. The programme of the last show is still written up in chalk on the walls!

There are, of course, a great many other buildings in the main part of the Dockyard. A large block, built c. 1855-57, containing the blacksmith's, coppersmith's, fitting and shipwright's shops, was pulled down to make space to store cars being imported to the Island during the early 1970s. Other workshops, the electricity generating station, and the gas factory, with its gas-holder, are still in existence, but in a generally dilapidated condition. Several fine storehouses and the workshops of the main complex are rented out to firms as storage space, most of them being kept in good repair by the firms concerned. These buildings, though of interest to the Yard as a whole, have no specific merits in themselves worthy of note.

One of the best known structures is the barracks, standing high above the south wall, and visible for many miles. This was originally built as the Ordnance Barracks, post-1829 and pre-1843, by the Army. Owing to its position close to the casemated south wall, it has for long been known as Casemates. The building has been used in its time for naval barracks, a Canadian Navy antisubmarine training school, a NAAFI provision store, and, more recently as Bermuda's high security prison.

All of the buildings in the Dockyard are constructed on a grand scale, such as can be found wherever the British built during the 19th century. The maximum use was made of local stone, but a great deal of granite was brought from England for steps, dock facings, etc. No expense seems to have been spared to ensure that the workmanship was of an exceptionally high standard, and it is thanks to this that these fine buildings are in such good general order today, since the maintenance on them has been sadly lacking in recent years.

The Victualling Yard

Until 1853, all victualling stores were held in the hulks *Royal Oak* and *Weymouth*, and these stores were made available to all personnel, service and civilian, convicts and freemen alike, employed in the Dockyard.

In the first instance, a site for this yard on the Admiralty-owned property at Spanish Point was suggested by an official in London, who obviously had no idea of the geography of the Island, the difficulty in

View of the Dockyard, 1857, by Le Marchant. This panorama gives a perfect picture of the layout of the buildings at this time, and is accurate even to the number of windows in each building. In the foreground is the Keep, with the Victualling Yard, and both the twin-towered new storehouse and the single-towered old storehouse showing clearly beyond. In the background is Casemates Barracks. A good idea of the massiveness of the fortifications is given by this view, which must have been painted from the lower balcony of Commissioner's House. (Reproduced by kind permission of Mr. Jay Bluck)

crossing the Staggs Channel, or of the problem of berthing on Spanish Point! Fortunately, this idea was swiftly vetoed by the local naval authorities.

However, as early as 1818, proposals were in hand for a Victualling Yard to be constructed on Ireland Island, the site chosen being the Spar Yard, which would in fact appear to have been a good choice. The complex would have had a large wharf giving directly on to the water, where boats could load up with stores and transship them direct to the ships at anchor in Grassy Bay. For some unknown reason, this plan was not carried into effect and alternative plans were later drawn up.

Although work is said to have commenced in 1827, a chart of 10 October 1829*, shows only a vague outline of the Victualling Yard area, with sketches of some of the proposed buildings, though these are not the actual ones eventually erected. This is hardly surprising since it was not completed until some twenty years later, by which time, no doubt, ideas on the architecture had considerably changed.

The position of the Victualling Yard ensures complete security from attack, so at least the authorities of the day could rest assured that had there been any action in Bermuda, the lime juice, flour and rum would have been the last to fall into enemy hands!

However in 1848, Lord Dundonald, the inveterate 'digger', proposed to the Admiralty that the area should be converted into a Spar Yard, and that tunnels should be dug under Maria Hill to take the victualling stores. This suggestion was shelved when it was found that the stone in Maria Hill was the hardest in Ireland Island and that the cost of excavating it would be phenomenal.

After several years under a system of unsuccessful Agent Victuallers on a salary of £400 per annum, Samuel Triscott was given the post. He was a most stormy man, who argued with everyone from the Commander-in-Chief down! However, he was obviously capable, and was socially very pleasant, and he held his position for nineteen years, just one year short of earning a salary of £600 per year! He was a keen yachtsman, and a founder of the Bermuda Native Yacht Club and the Royal Bermuda Yacht Club.

Careening and Docking Facilities

The great benefit of Bermuda's geographical position in the western Atlantic has always been that it provides a base where ships can be repaired without having to make the long journey back to England, or northwards

---

* Admiralty Chart No. A 824, dated 10th October, 1829 (not reproduced)

to the inferior and often ice-bound dockyard at Halifax, Nova Scotia. It was therefore one of the main objects of the Dockyard to provide facilities for careening and major repair work, particularly to underwater damage.

In the very earliest plans for the Dockyard (1811), careening pits and capstans are shown in position to the south of the Camber, then known as Ireland Cove. There is also a record of pits being dug in St. George's just prior to this date; Admiralty Island having been bought specifically for this purpose.

There was considerable dialogue between the Admiralty and the local naval authorities concerning the digging for a dry dock, and a chart of 1818* shows the originally proposed site for such a dock, in what was a very small camber. Again, a chart of 1826-29**, which shows the camber area extended to the area of the present North Yard, included a dock built into land which had to be reclaimed to form the Great Wharf. However, the Admiralty on both occasions ruled that the porosity of the local stone made it unsuitable for the building of a dry dock, and ordered the installation of careening capstans to the north of the camber. These capstans, had cast in the top surface 'Invented by T. Millwright 1828, Manufactured H.M. Dockyard Portsmouth, 1831'. Capstans and pits are marked on a Chart of 1856*** in this area, together with a 'temporary, Careening Gear Shed'.

It is appropriate here to explain the use of these pits. The term 'careening' means the scraping of the underwater section of the ship's bottom to clear it from barnacles, weed etc., and to repair and make watertight the seams and holes made by marine borers which could not otherwise be reached for this purpose. In order to do this, it was necessary to haul down (tilt) the ship to one side until half of the ship's bottom was raised out of the water, so that the crew could clean-off and effect the repairs. When one side was finished, the ship would be hauled down the other way, so the process could be repeated for the other half of the bottom.

Although a ship's yardarms, the lateral spars from which the sails are suspended, could be 'trained' a certain distance fore-and-aft, this was not sufficient for careening purposes, and to avoid having to 'strike' (lower) the yardarms, pits were dug ashore into which the ends of the yardarms could be lowered, thus enabling the ship to be heeled at a greater angle, and expose more of the bottom for cleaning. The support given to the ship by the yardarms was also useful in avoiding the danger of the ship capsizing during this process. Of course, the capstans were used to haul the ships over

---

* Admiralty Chart A 822 of 30th April, 1818 (see page 8)

** Admiralty Chart A 825 (undated; not reproduced)

*** Admiralty Chart D 8101 of 20th May, 1856 (not reproduced)

to this rather ungainly position by the use of ropes secured to the masts.

A definite decision not to continue with the scheme for a dry dock was taken on several occasions. In 1842, the subject came up again, and in 1860, a further attempt was made to put forward proposals for a dry dock, drawings for which still exist*. This time the proposal was contained in a complete plan for the extension of the Dockyard to the area now covered by the South Yard, which is shown as incorporating a 250-foot long dry dock in the area just to the south of the short arm. This plan was again quashed by the Admiralty, which is unfortunate, since this particular design of the entrance to the Dockyard would have protected the harbour from the easterly winds which cause very unpleasant conditions inside the breakwater.

The first mention of a floating dock was made in 1852, but arguments still went on until 1862, with nothing being decided. Eventually, it is not clear who made the decision, the situation was clarified by the building by Messrs. Campbell, Johnson & Co., of a floating dock at their Blackwall yard, North Woolwich, London. This dock, measuring 380 x 124 x 72 feet was the largest in the world at that time, and was designed to lift 10,000 tons. It cost £250,000.

The dock was towed from Sheerness to Bermuda by four of the Royal Navy's largest ironclads. *Northumberland* and *Agincourt* took it as far as Porto Santo, Madeira, and it was towed from there to Bermuda by *Warrior* and *Black Prince*, each furnished with 1,000 tons of coal. The *Terrible* guided the stern for the entire journey. After a 35-day passage, the dock, appropriately named *Bermuda*, arrived on 28 July 1869. She was moored submerged in Grassy Bay until April of the following year, when she was moved into the camber without incident.

Having been moved into the North Camber in April 1870, the dock served well until about 1904. In fact, its availability in Bermuda was of more importance to the Navy than the rest of the facilities in the Island! During the hurricane of 1878, it was considerably damaged, even though the precaution of 'flooding-down' (sinking) had been taken.

By 1900, it was realised that the dock was too small for the new generation of ships, and *Bermuda* was sold to a German firm shortly before the outbreak of World War I. The firm partly dismantled the dock in situ, but were so slow that it was towed across to Spanish Point so that its berth could be used for naval vessels. Its demolition was interrupted by the war, and never recommenced, and its remains can still be seen off Spanish Point. There was much conjecture at the time that the Germans were more

* Admiralty Chart A 5568 of 15th March, 1860 (not reproduced)

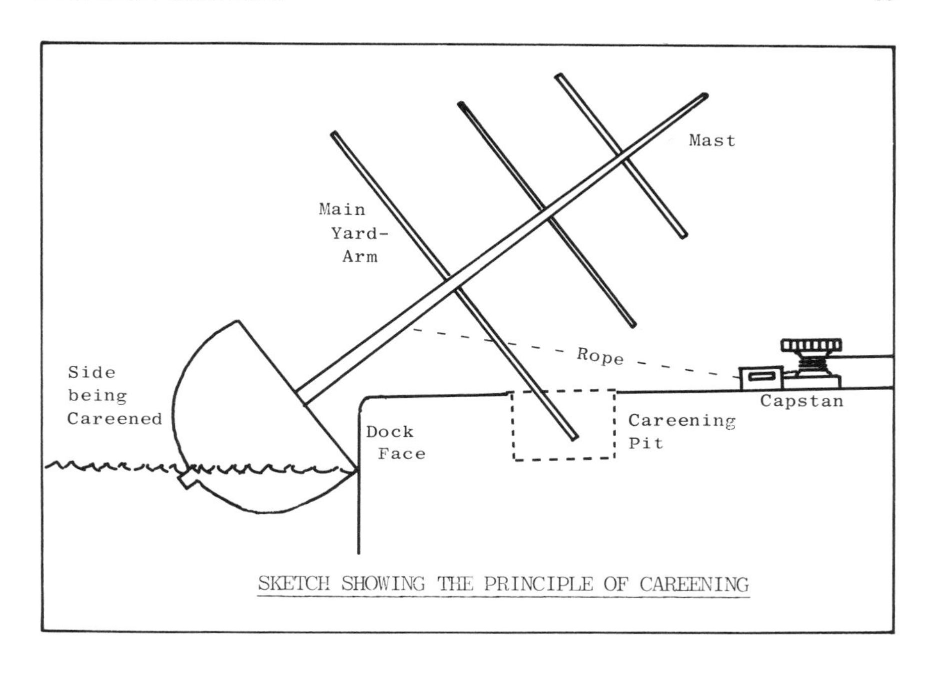

SKETCH SHOWING THE PRINCIPLE OF CAREENING

Early photograph showing the first floating dock Bermuda *and giving a good impression of its size. HMS* Bellerophon *in dock* (Godsiff)

interested in finding out details of the channel to the Dockyard than in the purchase of the dock, as their representatives spent a great deal of time out fishing in the main fairway, when not actually engaged in dismantling the dock. In any case, they were not seen to catch many fish, nor were any serious attempts made to the demolish the remains of the dock.

A replacement dock had been ordered at a cost of £265,000. Again, it was the largest in the world at that time, measuring 545 x 100 feet internal beam, and was built by Messrs. Swan and Hunter, being launched on 8 February 1901. It left Sheerness on 11 July 1902, under tow by two Dutch tugs, there being no tugs powerful enough for the job in England at that time. It was considerably delayed by bad weather en route, the local newspapers becoming quite anxious as to its fate, but eventually it arrived on 8 August 1902, the day before the Coronation of King Edward VII. Interest locally was divided between preparations for the celebrations and the arrival of the Dock. Travelling via the Azores, the journey had taken fifty-three days, the weather not having been as favourable as in 1869.

Five tugs were used to bring the huge dock through the Narrows and up the channel, a worrying moment being when a gust of wind caused it to veer sharply when just about to leave the Narrows for Murray's Anchorage, but the tugs managed to regain control just in time. Boss's Cove was used as a temporary mooring place until the completion of the berth specially made for the dock in the new South Basin, which was not ready for it until 1905, owing to the problem of obtaining labour to complete the work.

One of the first occasions the dock, known as *Admiralty Floating Dock (AFD) No. 1*, was put to the test was when it was required to lift the 17,500-ton battleship HMS *Dominion*, after she had grounded and sustained considerable damage to her hull in the Gulf of St. Lawrence. The dock was only designed to lift 15,000 tons, and representatives from Swan Hunter & Co. of Newcastle-upon-Tyne were sent out to supervise the lift. It was the first time such a large vessel had been bodily lifted out of the water after launching, and proved the practicability of the floating dock system.

It was in fact the success of this lift which caused Admiral Jackie Fisher to reverse his decision to do away with the Dockyard at Bermuda, and reduce it to care and maintenance, as it clearly indicated the value of a floating dock in the western Atlantic.

Bermudians looked upon the dock with the same confidence with which they looked at the appearance of shark oil and the sound of the South Shore breakers in assessing the likelihood of a hurricane. The sinking of the dock was a sure indication that very severe weather was imminent, especially in the case of an expected hurricane.

The dock remained in Bermuda until 1946, when it was sold to a firm in

Montevideo, Uraguay, being replaced by *AFD No.5*, which had been towed out from Alexandria, Egypt. It was in this dock that HMS *Barham* (?), which was under repair at the time, had been severely damaged by the German forces in 1940.

AFD No.5 was not placed in its position in South Basin until 1948, having spent the previous two years moored off Frank's Bay, Southampton, ships being sent down to Port Royal in order to take advantage of the maintenance facilities she afforded. The depth of the water there enabled even heavy cruisers, such as HMS *Sheffield*, to be docked during this period.

After only a short period of service in Bermuda, on 11 July 1951, *AFD No.5* was towed to England by the two Navy tugs, *Warden* and *Reward*, its departure marking the final stage in the reduction of the Dockyard from its former glory. It was later moored in the River Fal, where it remained for an eighteen month refit before being recommissioned for further use in Home Waters.

The fourth floating dock to be used in Bermuda was *AFD No.48*, which was moored in the North Basin in December 1941, after it was purchased by the British Supply Council in the United States to supplement *AFD No.1.* After many years of service, in 1972, by then the property of the Bermuda government, it had deteriorated to such an extent that it was not possible to tow it far and it was sunk just to the west of Commissioners Point, in a 9-fathom deep, where it can still be seen on a clear day, making a fine home for the many beautiful fish which abound in that area.

It is of interest that during World War II a total of 572 ships were docked for repairs in *AFD No. 1* and *AFD No.48*, which gives some indication of the importance and use made of this facility.

One thing which is not often realised about floating docks is that they themselves occasionally need underwater repairs and careening. The dock *Bermuda* had to be careened by being tilted sideways, much as the old sailing ships had to be hauled down. However, *AFD No. 1* was far more sophisticated, being designed to 'dock herself'! This was possible since the dock was constructed in three sections, which were detachable from each other.

To undertake the careening, the centre (bottom) of the dock was raised in relation to the sides, which were designed to support the full weight of the empty dock. The bottom was then scraped by sending a team of men underneath on flat rafts. Once this had been done, the bottom was painted, and then lowered back into the water. Next, one side was raised and careened in a similar manner, followed by the other side, on completion of which the dock was ready for further service.

The sheerlegs (right) with the floating dock Bermuda. (Godsiff)

The Sheerlegs and 80-ton Crane

The requirement for a heavy lift capability in the Dockyard was recognised in 1873, and the following year, James Taylor and Co, of Birkenhead, commenced fabrication of a pair of sheerlegs for shipment and erection in Bermuda in 1875.

The specification for these sheerlegs was for a 90-foot clearance at thirty feet outward lean, giving a total height above datum of 100 feet. They were constructed from half inch steel plate, about three feet in diameter. The legs were approximately twenty-five feet apart. The whole structure, including backstays and counter-weights, weighed some 195 tons.

Erection of the sheerlegs was a masterpiece of ingenuity. The old *Irresistible* was brought into use, and the sheerlegs were loaded on to the bow, supported by means of eighty foot spars, installed for the purpose. The *Irresistible* was then hauled out across the basin and positioned so that the heel of each leg lined up with the cast iron steps (large steel hinges), let into the wharf surface, which are still visible, after which the backstays were used to hoist the sheerlegs to an upright position.

After fifty-five years service, on 21 February 1930, the sheerlegs were struck at a ceremony by many local dignitaries; among the guests was the Lady Scott-Montague of Beaulieu, who happened to be staying with the Captain of the Dockyard and Mrs. Holt. Also attending was Mr. Johnny Lee, who had joined the Dockyard as a boy on a paddle tug in October 1859, and who was known as the 'Dockyard Encyclopaedia'. He had assisted at the setting up of the sheerlegs, and was offered the job of cutting the backstays with an acetylene torch, but refused on the grounds, that he 'did not hold with these new-fangled pieces of equipment'!

Lowering the sheerlegs was achieved by cutting through the legs with an oxy-acetylene torch, then at the right moment similarly cutting through the backstays, when the sheerlegs fell with a great splash into the harbour. It is of interest that the huge sheerlegs at Gibraltar were felled by a similar method in December 1973.

Thus disappeared a landmark, which for over fifty years had been used by seamen approaching Bermuda from the northward. The replacement, an 80-ton lift crane, was already in position in the South Yard. It was constructed by Messrs Stothert and Pitt in 1926, and was dismantled in the early 1980s.

Admiralty House viewed from off Clarence Cove (FKS)

5

Residences

Admiralty House

From 1795 until 1806, the Commander-in-Chief was housed in St. George's. A move was then made to Langton Hill, though it appears that this house was never, in fact, occupied, followed in 1810 by Mount Wyndham at Bailey's Bay, which had the advantage of a good view across to St. George's Harbour and also to Ireland Island, so the Commander-in-Chief could keep in touch with both harbours, by means of his semaphore-equipped Signal Station. A long-term lease was signed between owner Stephen Outerbridge and the Commander-in-Chief, Sir John Borlase Warren on 27 December, 1812.

With the build up of Ireland Island, and the closing down of St. George's as a naval depot, the requirement to overlook that harbour lapsed and it was considered more convenient to move the Commander-in-Chief's residence nearer to the Dockyard.

It so happened that St. John's Hill, which had been rented for a naval hospital, was being vacated at that time, and had been put up for sale. It seemed a suitable building, and was accordingly purchased by the Colonial Government, along with an adjoining lot in 1816. After extensive repairs, which brought the total sum expended to £2,000, the Government presented the whole property to the Crown in perpetuity as a residence for the Commander-in-Chief of the naval station with headquarters in Bermuda. Additional land was purchased over the next several years and added to the gift, which eventually totalled in excess of twenty-two acres.

It is difficult to say with any certainty who was the first Commander-in-Chief to take up residence at St. John's Hill, as Rear Admiral Sir David

Milne preferred Mount Wyndham, where he entertained the Lieutenant Governor of Nova Scotia in 1818, and where he continued to reside until he left Bermuda in 1819.

St. John's Hill was still in need of considerable repair, no doubt due in part to a hurricane which caused a great deal of damage. However, little money was forthcoming, and a committee was formed to propose alterations and repairs.

In 1821, Admiral Fahie added some wine cellars to preserve his health and that of his suite. However, further shortcomings were the subject of another survey board, which stated it was not a fit residence for a Commander-in-Chief. Nevertheless, the Commander-in-Chief remained in residence there until 1956.

Extra rooms were proposed in 1828, but the house was said to be unfit to be extended. Small wonder if the Commander-in-Chief was angry about the money being sunk into the Commissioner's House, for his Dockyard counterpart at that very same time! A further attempt to improve the area was made in 1844, when the convict hulk *Resolute,* with thirty convicts onboard, was moved and moored off Boss's Cove, a right-of-way being paid for to enable the convicts to get to work daily. A plot of ground was levelled, but there was no building carried out. No plans exist of this proposed extension, but according to Admiral Austin it was to have been a magnificent structure.

When Lord Dundonald was Commander-in-Chief, (1848-50), he arranged to have caves tunnelled through the soft rock for transporting stores and to give temporary stowage in a cool and even temperature for his household requirements. A tunnel was also cut under the road to the kitchen garden. It is said that banquets were held by candle-light in the larger caves, which must have made a picturesque setting. These tunnels were dug largely by miners from the Durham area, who were serving in the prison hulks.

The existing estate was completed by Sir Houston Steward in 1859, but the house was too small for the staff, and the Flagship was anchored off Clarence Cove to accommodate them. The cove, originally called Abbott's Bay, had been renamed in 1830 when H.R.H. the Duke of Clarence ascended the throne as William IV - popularly known as the 'Sailor King'. At the same time Admiralty House was renamed Clarence House, and the hill on which it stood, Clarence Hill.

Between 1898 and 1956, there were virtually no changes to Admiralty House, the ballroom having been added in 1897. The last Commander-in-Chief to reside in Admiralty House was Vice Admiral Sir John Eaton, whose flag was lowered at sunset on 30 October 1956, when he sailed to

Norfolk, Virginia to take up the post of Deputy Chief, NATO.

In 1957, shortly after the last of the Royal Navy personnel had left, six police officers volunteered to move into Admiralty House as caretakers. Others followed, and for five years the Police enjoyed the amenities of both the house and its grounds. The Bermuda Regiment was headquartered at the house from 1962 until 1972, when the Regiment moved to Warwick Camp, taking the huge mast and yard-arm with them.

To the dismay of a great many people, the house, with the exception of the ballroom was purposely burned down on 24 January 1974. After plans to build the hotel school on the grounds were defeated by public outcry, the area was declared a public park in 1975.

Commissioner's House

Up to 1809, no permanent naval officer was appointed in charge of the Dockyard areas. The first Superintendent, Captain Andrew Evans, who held the post from 1811-17, lived in an existing cottage on the slope on the northeast side of Ireland Cove from 1816. In 1817, the title of 'Commissioner' was officially approved, and Captain John Lewis was appointed to this post. Captain Lewis came to Bermuda from the Dockyard in Antigua when that establishment closed, bringing some equipment with him.

In 1823 the building of the Commissioner's House was commenced as a 'Residence suitable for the dignity of the post'. The original residence of the Commissioner was eventually destroyed in the course of excavating around the cove. Construction continued with varying degrees of urgency until completion in 1829.

The Commissioners, who were members of the Lords Commissioners of the Admiralty in London were:

Captain John Lewis	1817-23
Captain Thomas Briggs	1823-29
Captain Charles Inglis	1829 (for a few months)
Captain J. Ayscough	1829-32
Captain Sir Thomas Ussher KCB	1832

The reason for Captain Ayscough's relief is of interest. Having served as Commissioner from 1829-32, he was unwise enough to feel secure in expressing his 'dismay at His Majesty's Mental Health and ... hoped that when he regained his health he would take steps to replace the reigning Government with one more capable' !

The reaction to this proves that not all letters are left lingering in in-trays. The next ship brought out Sir Thomas Ussher to take over as a Commissioner, even though this title only lasted for a few more months. In

1832, the title lapsed and was changed to 'Commodore Superintendent' and Ussher continued as the commodore superintendent until 1837, when he was transferred to Halifax. At this time, the Commissioner's House was handed over to the Army.

His successor lived in The Cottage, a former house on the present site, which remained the residence of the Superintendent/Captain-in-Charge/ Resident Naval Officer, in sequence until 1968, when it became the residence of the Senior Naval Officer, West Indies. The present Cottage dates from 1938.

The costs of building the Commissioner's House have never accurately been assessed, but caused a great deal of anxiety and recrimination at the time. Mahogany was used throughout; the stairs are said to have been of marble, and as mentioned below, the verandahs were of Yorkshire paving stone. There was, so the story runs, a marble bath which cost £5000 with its extravagant fittings, and all the modern refinements of hot and cold running water. Parts of this system were allegedly seen rotting and rusting at the rear of the building in 1855. Suffice it to say that in 1933 there were only two bathrooms on the upper floor, small and mediocre, and but one 'by means of a paraffin heater, and often at hazard to life and limb, could supply hot water'. Such is progress!

In 1826 the Dockyard reported the cost to date as:

Materials and Labour	£30,550
'incidentals'	6,110
	£36,660

It is hardly surprising that in 1827 the Admiralty ordered an investigation into the improvident expenditure of £42,511, and at the same time stopped all future spending on the house. As a result, in 1828, a stop was put on the supply of Yorkshire paving stones for the balconies. However, after considerable bickering, in 1830, these paving stones were sent to Bermuda, and installed!

The enquiry was drawn out and totally inconclusive. In June 1828, the Commissioners reported that £16,000 of the £42,000 in question had wrongly been attributed to the cost of the house. However, this still left some £26,000 to be accounted for on a building whose original cost was estimated at £12,400! One interesting feature of the enquiry was that certain items, costed at £4,000 in England, were charged for at £28,000 in Bermuda!

In 1837, the post of Commodore Superintendent was abolished, and the job was taken over by a Naval Storekeeper, Mr. Ballingall, who became the Superintendent, a post he held for a total of thirty years, during which time he was allowed only three months' leave! When he left in 1857, Captain Hutton took over, becoming the first of a long line of Captains-in-Charge.

The original Commissioner's House (left), with its replacement under construction (right), circa 1822. The hill to the left, and the buildings on it, were later razed to prepare the site for the Victualling Yard and to provide fill the building of the Breakwater. (Driver, 1821)

Commissioner's House, 1863, with Royal Marines on the balcony. Note the ventilation holes, often mistaken for gunports, which ensured that the cellars of the house remained well-cooled even during the heat of summer. (J.B. Heyl)

The Cottage in 1965. Built in 1938, this building replaced the original Cottage which stood on the same site. Note Victoria Row in the background.

Eventually the total costs apparently rose to a fantastic £56,000, which excluded the cost of items supplied from England, such as doors, window-frames, etc! Lord Dundonald, when desperately trying to obtain a few hundred pounds for essential repairs to Admiralty House in 1848, sent a very succinct letter to the Admiralty, which included a passage saying that he 'failed to understand the requirement for accommodation for 11 stalled horses, and 2 Coach Houses on an Island only 1 mile long and unapproachable except by sea' - a most understandable comment !

In 1862, 112 Royal Marines were barracked in Commissioner's House, and it was also used from 1864-67 as a military staff office. During World War I, families were moved in for a while, when the house became a 'married quarter' but in 1919 it was returned to the Royal Navy and was commissioned as HMS *Malabar* VI, remaining as such until it was finally abandoned in 1951. The controversial stables were for many years used as the main NAAFI Store and Canteen.

Some idea of the size of this building and its outhouses can be obtained from the fact that in 1930 it housed nine Officers and 200 ratings, as well as being the office accommodation for HMS *Malabar*. Unfortunately since 1951 it has received no maintenance and is now in a very dilapidated condition. Only costly renovations can now save this historic building from ruin.

Dockyard Employees Houses

Most of the original residences were built on the slopes below where the Commissioner's House now stands, but during the construction of the fortifications, the hill was blasted and the rocks used as fill for the construction works. Certainly the Master Attendant, the Boatswain of the Yard, and the Foreman of the Yard, lived there until 1827, after which they were probably accommodated in the hulk *Royal Oak* , at least until their official residences were built.

In 1827, the original Cottage was built, and in the same year Captain Fanshawe, Royal Engineers, commenced work on the major fortifications around Commissioner's Point, a job which was never really finished. By 1842, all military personnel, except the Royal Engineers, had been withdrawn from the area.

The year 1840 saw the beginning of Prince Alfred Terrace, the Dockyard medical officer occupying No.1, which had a fish pond in the grounds to ensure a plentiful supply of fresh fish for his table. The rest of the block was added between 1864 and 1867.

At first, very few Dockyard officers were provided with residences. After much argument and discussion, a row of houses, known as Dockyard

Terrace, was commenced north of the camber in 1849. These were allocated to such persons as the master attendant, the foreman of the Victualling Yard, and the engineer of the yard. By this time, all other private residents were obliged to live outside the Dockyard in an area beyond the Cut Bridge.

The Terrace houses were never popular, as they backed against the wall of the Victualling Yard, so had no rear windows, which tended to make them damp. However, they form a most distinguished row of houses whose gardens, in their heyday, formed a most attractive addition to the Dockyard scene, and their view of the activities of the Dockyard must have been second to none.

Up until 1842, the artisans employed in the Dockyard were housed in wooden huts in the North Yard. In 1849, Victoria Row was built for them: no one knows where they lived for the seven years in between! Lodge Point was also built in 1849, but was transferred to the War Department in 1859. This block remained under the War Department until 1922, with the exception of Nos. 3 and 6, which were for some reason retained for use by naval families.

In 1866, Captain J.F. Grant hit on the idea of building a block of single men's quarters for the young apprentices and technicians. This was constructed on Maria Hill, but does not appear to have been a great success, as the problem of supervision was never really overcome. After the closure of the Dockyard, the building was used as a chicken farm for some years, and subsequently as a pig farm, before being completely abandoned.

There were of course many other houses built for the families of civilian Dockyard workers: Portland Place being the first, followed by Albert Row, and extensions to Victoria Row, Clarence Terrace, and Princess Louise Terrace. These most unattractive rows of houses, typical of their kind during that period, are still being usedas rental units.

Other buildings overlooking Cockburn's Cut, were occupied by the Army from 1817-53. These became filthy, dilapidated hovels towards the end of their life, but the occupants clung on to their possessions, and despite many attempts to evict them, the houses could not be pulled down for many years.

In 1938, with the threat of war, there was an influx of an additional 200 civilian personnel to augment the Dockyard staff, and a mess was built on Watford Island to provide recreation and accommodation facilities for them. This mess remained in use until 1951, when it was sold to the Bermuda Government. It is now in use as the Somerset Police Officer's Mess.

In 1963, the new naval policy of providing its personnel with married quarters was extended to Bermuda. Prince Alfred Terrace was rescued from a dilapidated state, and converted into 10 apartments for ratings and their families. No.1 was allocated as a Prison Officer's Mess for officers employed by the Bermuda Government at the prison, which was at that time moved from Hamilton to the Casemates Barracks, in the Dockyard.

From 1972 onwards, it became a condition of service that only married naval personnel, accompanied by their families, could be appointed to Bermuda, the officers, and those ratings not fortunate enough to be housed in Prince Alfred Terrace, were obliged to rent houses in the vicinity. The only residences provided by the Navy were The Cottage (Senior Naval Officer West Indies), Magazine House (Resident Naval Officer) and No.4 South Road (Radio Supervisor).

6

Other Naval Properties

RN Hospitals, Bermuda

Prior to 1812, there was no Royal Naval Hospital in Bermuda, and a cabin-flat in the hulk *Tourterelle*, moored in St. George's Harbour, was used for this purpose. In 1812, several islands in the Great Sound - Ports, Hawkins and Long Islands - were considered with the aim of erecting a hospital. However, nothing came of this scheme for a long time.

In the meanwhile, St. John's Hill was still rented by the Admiralty, but was not in use. With the yellow fever outbreak in that year, this house was used as a hospital. Twenty-eight died there during this epidemic.

In 1814, the hulk *Romulus* was commissioned and moored off Spanish Point as a hospital ship for ratings. St. John's Hill became the officers' hospital at the same time, and remained as such until it was taken over as Admiralty House two years later.

In the meantime, application was made for approval to build a proper naval hospital on Ireland Island. This was granted, and the hospital was opened in June 1818. It was a grand place, having four wards of twenty beds each, but from 1818-26, there was no provision at all for officers, who, with the loss of St. John's Hill, had to be placed in lodgings when sick.

The West Wing was added in 1826, incorporating a small officers' ward, and in 1827, the East Wing, designed for officers, was completed. A second storey was added to both wings in 1860.

In 1834, a Quarantine Hospital was established on Ports Island. Between 1852 and 1869, this was used by personnel from many ships. It was, of course, used largely to isolate yellow fever patients. An indication of the virulence of that dread disease can be gauged from the following story:

RN Hospital, Bermuda, from the Crawl (1823). The Hospital Inspector General's residence (since demolished) can be seen on the left. (Driver)

The Zymotic Hospital for treatment of infectious diseases, today known as Lefroy House.

Men off the *Barracouta* suffering from yellow fever were housed in one wing of the building. When the epidemic died down, the wing lay undisturbed for about one year, until a party of Royal Marines was sent to repair it. All of these men contracted yellow fever, presumably through bites from infected mosquitos; two died almost at once, as did the doctor who was accompanying the rest of the party to Halifax for treatment!

After this horrible experience, the ward was burnt to the ground and never rebuilt. Ports Island is now used as a youth centre by the Bermuda Government.

The Naval Hospital served the Dockyard faithfully right up until 1951, when it was sold as a part of the closing-down deal to the Bermuda Government. From that time it lay idle, until it was reduced to the ignominy of becoming a chicken farm. In November 1972, it was so infested with rats and its condition was so dangerous that the Fire Department burned it to the ground.

Close to the main hospital, but built right on the water's edge near to Grey's Bridge, was the Isolation Hospital, built in 1899 as a replacement to the Ports Island Hospital and known as the 'Zymotic'. In 1952, the Committee of Twenty-Five extensively renovated the building, opening it as a children's hospital. More recently, it has been used as a home for Senior Citizens, who for the most part require nursing care, under the name of Lefroy House.

The Dockyard Chapel

Despite the Dockyard buildings having been commenced in 1812, no church or chapel was built for many years. Services were held in one of the storehouses, but not many attended as it was too far for people to come, particularly as there was no chaplain!

In 1823, the Reverend and Mrs. Ellison, possibly Elliston, came out with the convicts. After two years service, he became a certified lunatic and was sent back to England! However he returned, but must have had a relapse, as he was again replaced in 1826 by a very sane and worldly man, the Reverend Bloxom.

It was during this period that the Parsonage was built, together with a small oratory, converted from a slave-hut, which held just enough people for early communion.

Despite continual applications by the superintendent, Mr. Ballingall, it was not until 1846 that Their Lordships intimated that funds would be forthcoming for a church, and in 1847 an enquiry was received as to how many sittings would be necessary.

The Dockyard Chapel, on the upper floor of No.2 Victualling Store. The last service was held on 3 September, 1950. (Source unknown)

The reply was that 800 were necessary, a very optimistic figure on the part of the Chaplain, and this made such an impression on Their Lordships that nothing further was heard from them until 1850, when Mr. Ballingall was asked if divine service could be held on the upper floor of No.2 Victualling Store.

He of course replied that this was utterly impossible, so by return post the order came back to 'make it so'. One half of the floor in question was to be fitted as a 'Chapel for Publick Worship'.

By 1852, the chapel was finished, with tablets containing the Commandments and the Apostles' Creed, which had been sent out from England, installed on either side of the altar. These tablets were lost, possibly to the Army Chapel of Boaz Island, and were later replaced by painted lettering. Similarly, an 'American Barell Organ' was installed, 'exhibited' is the word used by Captain Carr (1892-94).

It seems that attendance was low at the chapel. No one could really expect workers who walked to the Dockyard some two and a half miles daily from Somerset, to come again on Sunday, when there were churches much nearer home. The Roman Catholics used the Foresters Hall, near the Lagoon, the Weslyans the only 'proper' Church which was purchased from

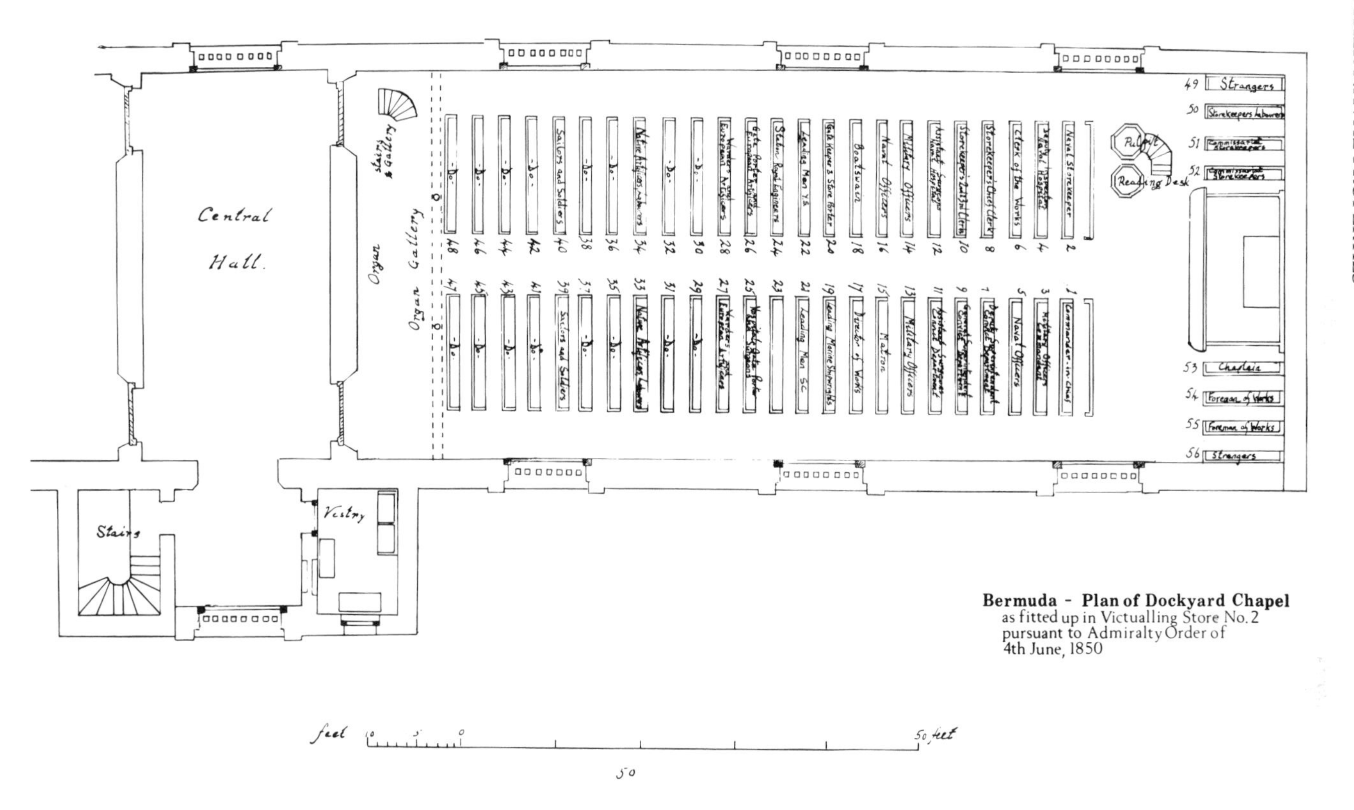

Bermuda - Plan of Dockyard Chapel
as fitted up in Victualling Store No. 2
pursuant to Admiralty Order of
4th June, 1850

them in 1960, and consecrated as 'All Saints' (Church of England). In the 1930s, a move was made to reactivate the military chapel on Boaz Island, but nothing came of this.

The Dockyard Church was finally abandoned in 1951, when the property was sold to the Bermuda Government. The organ was packed and shipped to England, where it was in use for a time at HMS *Excellent*, but has since been replaced. At the same time, the altar, pulpit and font, were transferred to Southampton Parish Church (St. Annes), the font later being placed in the Chapel of Ease at Horseshoe Bay. The plaque in memory of those who drowned in HMS *Valerian*, in 1926, was built into the wall of the Emmanuel Methodist Church, Southampton.

The King's Colour of the West Indies Station

By command of King George V, King's Colours were first given to the Royal Navy in 1924. Initially, eight such colours were presented to the three Home Commands of Chatham, Portsmouth and Plymouth, the Home and Mediterranean Fleets, and the East Indies, South Atlantic, and America and West Indies Stations. More recently, a Colour was presented to the Far East Station, and in 1956, Her Majesty the Queen presented her Colour to the Fleet Air Arm. Colours are also held by the Canadian Naval Forces at Halifax and Esquimalt; by the Royal Australian Navy, and the Royal New Zealand Navy.

The Colour is a white ensign of silk with a crown and royal cypher, superimposed with a blue and gold cord and tassels. It is carried on an ash staff surmounted by a gilt badge consisting of an admiralty-pattern anchor on a three-faced shield with a crown superimposed.

The Colour, which can either be termed the King's Colour or the Queen's Colour, the name depending on the monarch, is only paraded when Royalty or their representatives are present; for foreign Sovereigns or Heads of State; for the Queen's Birthday Parade; and other important ceremonial occasions as ordered by the Admiralty. It is never paraded on board ships, nor in foreign territory.

On the America and West Indies Station, there have been three King's Colours. The first, bearing the Royal Cypher of King George V, is now in St. James' Church, Sandys, where it was laid-up in 1953, during a ceremony in which the guard and band of HMS *Sheffield* took part. Prior to this time, the Colour had been kept firstly in the Dockyard Chapel, and then, from March, 1951, when the Chapel was de-consecrated, in The Cottage, under the custody of the Resident Naval Officer.

The second, bearing the cypher of King George VI, was laid up on 23

December 1951 at St. John's Church Pembroke. The latest Colour, which, by command of Queen Elizabeth II also bears the cypher of King George VI, was brought out from the United Kingdom in HMS *Sheffield* in 1953.

Other flagships of the America and West Indies Station which have carried this Colour are:

HMS *Superb*	1952-53
HMS *Sheffield*	1953-54
HMS *Superb*	1954-55
HMS *Kenya*	1955- April, 1956

From the latter date, the colour was kept at Admiralty House until 28 October 1956, when it was laid up during a ceremony at the Cathedral of the Holy Trinity, Hamilton, twenty-four hours prior to the final departure of the Commander-in-Chief, America and West Indies Station from Bermuda for the last time, in HMS *Bigbury Bay* .

The Lagoon

There is a legend which says that the Lagoon fed from the Crawl was flooded to bury a large number of yellow fever victims. However this cannot be substantiated since in 1814, Commodore Evans ordered a timber-carrying ship to offload masts there, and in 1815, ordered that 'on the approach of the hurricane month all Gunboats and Yard Craft not in use should be secured in the bays at Ports Island and, on any indication of bad weather the launches, flats and boats are to be promptly removed from the Dockyard and secured in the old Mast Pond and Crawle'. Moreover, a Spanish map of 1694 clearly shows that there was natural access even at that time.

However, a map of 1825 shows that a causeway had been built across the southeast end of the Lagoon, and by 1843 the stagnant water had become a perfect breeding place for the *Aedis aegypti* mosquito, now known to be the carrier of the dreaded yellow fever. Sentries posted in that area during that terrible year all died from yellow fever, but even so, it was not until 1849 that anyone considered the stagnant Lagoon to be a health hazard.

In 1849, Lord Dundonald ordered an investigation into the Lagoon as a result of which, decomposed and decaying matter some three feet thick was found there! An Admiralty letter of July 1849 ordered the causeway to be opened, and this was replaced with a small bridge shortly afterwards.

However, the Lagoon continued to smell and, at long last, an enlightened doctor suggested that it might have an influence on the number of yellow fever outbreaks. A further thorough investigation, by the Works Department, discovered that the graves of six yellow fever victims nearby were awash at high tide, hence the legend, no doubt. A convict, who happened to be a civil engineer, is thought to have proposed the answer to the problem, and as a result of his recommendations, a cut was made through the land to the northwestern end of the Lagoon in 1850.

This ensured a reasonable flow through the Lagoon, but in turn caused considerable silting of the whole area, which is now only a few inches deep, though no longer stagnant.

The Foresters' Hall, by the northwest entrance to the Lagoon, was built by the artisans in 1857. It was later used as a place of worship by the Roman Catholics, but eventually fell into disrepair. It has recently (1973) been allocated to the Somerset Unit of the Bermuda Sea Cadet Corps, as a headquarters.

Royal Naval Cemeteries

The RN Cemetery in the Glade, Ireland Island, was consecrated in 1812. Until 1853, all persons, naval and civilian, could be buried there, but thereafter only service personnel were permitted to be interred in this area.

In 1849, the convicts were ousted to Watford Island, as it was not thought propitious to bury them close to sailors! There are said to be over 400 convicts buried in the Watford Cemetery, but the size of the graveyard seems to preclude their having been buried in consecrated ground. A few

The Cemetery in the Glade, with the Oration Stand (since demolished) and tombstones which include those in memory of four Commanders-in Chief.

are also said to be buried in the 'convicts' Graveyard' just opposite the main naval cemetery, on the west shore of Ireland Island, but few headstones are inscribed to confirm this, and some are thought to be those of suicides. This graveyard dates from 1822, with most of the graves being dated from 1838 to 1843. There is no indication that this graveyard has ever been consecrated.

In 1854, Governor Elliott asked the Admiralty for permission to use Long Island as an overflow graveyard, since the yellow fever epidemics had caused all the available space in the Glade to be used up. From that time, Long Island was used for all epidemic deaths, convicts or freemen. The following figures show why yellow fever was so dreaded. These are from the hospital records of the time:

Year	Total Infected	% Deaths
1812	112	25
1818	105	21
1819	106	23
1837	138	16
1843	1047	11
1853	138	21
1856	68	12
1864	295	23

In 1853, the Inspector General of the hospital and his deputy both died. Fear was so great after the dreadful epidemic of 1843 that during the next outbreak in 1853, 25 September was appointed as a day of humiliation and prayer; all work in the Dockyard was stopped from 0900-1500 so everyone could go to church. 3 January 1854, was observed as a day of thanksgiving. There has been no yellow fever in Bermuda since 1884.

According to unpublished papers, dysentery was as virulent in its effects as yellow fever; the other two killer diseases were in order, phthisis (tuberculosis) and DTs.

The cemetery on Long Island contains the graves of many yellow fever victims, including two doctors who died at their posts in 1864. It was not consecrated until 1903.

There are many interesting, and some pathetic, headstones in the Glade. Among others, four Commanders-in-Chief rest there:

- Vice Admiral Sir Edward G-Colpoys, KCB d. 9 Nov, 1832, aged 67
- Vice Admiral the Hon. Sir Charles Paget d.29 Jan, 1839, aged 61 from Yellow Fever, whilst en route from Port Royal, Jamaica, to Bermuda, in HMS *Tartarus*

- Vice Admiral Sir Thomas Harvey, KCB, d.28 May, 1841, aged 66 at Clarence House
- Vice Admiral Sir T B W Napier, KCB, MVO d.30 Jul, 1920 ,aged 53 at Clarence House

The first Commissioner, Captain John Lewis, met tragedy in his family when he lost his two daughters, Ann and Mary, on 24 and 25 October 1819, together with his sister-in-law, who also died on 25 October, presumably from yellow fever which was rife in that year. He seems to have led a charmed life himself, as his clerk died almost a year later to the day! Nor were later holders of the post immune from the unhealthy climate of the time. One daughter of Mr. Ballingall, who was Superintendent of the Dockyard for 30 years, died in 1831, at the tender age of eleven months.

It is perhaps indicative of the perils of serving in the Navy at that time that a great number of deaths by drowning, falling from aloft and disease are recorded, mostly relating to people in what would nowadays be described as the prime of life, under thirty years of age.

Bridges

There are four bridges in the area in which we are interested, but it must be remembered that in the early years of the naval base there was no physical connection between Ireland Island and Boaz Island (the sea passage being known as Ireland Narrows), nor between Watford Island and Somerset (Somerset Narrows).

All the bridges north of Somerset were originally the property of the War Department. With the withdrawal of the Army from the West End, the bridges were transferred to the Admiralty on 1 January 1930. The bridges were returned to the War Department for legal purposes on 31 August 1951, prior to their final transfer to the Bermuda Government under the agreement of 1 February 1954.

Cockburn Cut

Cockburn Cut, spanned by the Cut Bridge, was named after the bay into which it opens on the eastern side, which was in turn called after the Commander-in-Chief (1832), Vice Admiral Sir George Cockburn, GCB. It was originally dug as part of a defensive ditch in 1817, but was later deemed to have been unnecessary, and was filled in again in 1823.

In 1843, a scheme to ship the quarried stone by barge from Moresby Plain to the Dockyard site caused the cut to be reopened, and a wooden structure was built to bridge the gap in 1845. By 1892, the wooden bridge was in bad condition and a poured concrete bridge was built to replace it.

The locals could not at first believe that a bridge made out of 'Porridge' could stand, and for a long time refused to cross it, preferring to row over by boat, or, if they were daring, cross one by one, to prevent overloading the span! The bridge is still in use today, proving how unfounded their fears were!

An interesting and amusing story is told about the area just to the east of Cockburn Cut. One day in 1913, the Dockyard medical officer, who lived in No. 1 Prince Alfred Terrace, was on his balcony relaxing after a hard day's work. He had even taken off his jacket, an unheard-of informality in those days, when he saw two cadets off one of the ships in Dockyard trying to cast off his boat, which was moored by the ferry dock.

He at once ran out of the house, without even waiting to put on his jacket, shouting all the time, and trying to attract the attention of the policeman on the Dockyard gate. This worthy eventually realised that something was amiss and leisurely strolled up the slope towards the bridge to see what was the matter. However, the irate doctor's shouts had already alerted the two cadets, who hurriedly jumped out of the boat to the shore, and ran up the steps to escape.

At this very moment, the late Horace Godsiff, then a young lad, who happened to be walking up the road on his way home from the Dockyard, passed the steps, and was very nearly knocked over by the two cadets, who dashed on towards the playing fields, where they could mingle with the many other cadets playing games. This may seem a not unusual story, but it takes on a great deal more interest when one learns that Mr. Godsiff recognised the two cadets concerned as Cadet Prince Albert of York, later King George VI of England, and his cadet companion! Needless to say, he kept their identity to himself, but ever since remembered that he is one of the few people in Bermuda to have been knocked flying by the future King of England.

Grey's Bridge

The next bridge to be constructed was Grey's Bridge, or more correctly 'The Grey Bridge', which was built by the Navy Works Department, on behalf of the Convict Department, to afford an easy access to Boaz Island, where the convict barracks was being built, from the Dockyard, where most of the convicts were housed in the hulks.

The bridge was opened by the Rt. Hon. the Earl of Dundonald on 1 January 1850, in an elaborate ceremony; an address being given in honour of the occasion by Mr. Anderson, the officer-in-charge of the work. The bridge was named 'The Grey Bridge, in honour of the Rt. Hon. Henry, Earl Grey, one of Her Majesty's Principal Secretaries of State', and not for Sir

Cockburn Cut, showing the mongram and date, 1892.

The Grey Bridge, built in 1850, showing the Deputy Inspector General's House (left), and the Zymotic Hospital (centre). (Godsiff)

Watford Bridge, showing the site of the horse ferry used until the construction of the first bridge at the turn of the century.

George Grey, Home Secretary, as has so often been misquoted. It has even been misspelt 'Gray'.

Grey's Bridge cost £680 to construct and remained in constant use until 1950, when it was replaced by the present inelegant causeway, constructed by the Navy Works Department, some ten yards to the west of the original site, just before the Dockyard closed. There is ample evidence in the poor finish of the upperworks of this bridge to indicate the final stages of construction were rushed to finish the work before the Navy relinquished responsibility for the area.

Little Watford Bridge

Little Watford Bridge, which was always known as the 'Piano Bridge' because of the rattling noise its rather loose planks made each time a vehicle crossed it, was built shortly after the Grey Bridge in order to join Boaz and Watford Islands together. After many refits, it was recommended for major overhaul in June 1954, owing to its dangerous condition. However, it was not until 7 June 1956, that £120,000 was voted for this work. In 1973, plans to replace this bridge by a causeway were put into effect, and during 1974 this landmark finally disappeared.

Watford Bridge

Shortly after the construction of the Grey Bridge and Little Watford Bridge, arrangements were made to maintain a constant communication across Somerset Narrows by means of a 'scow', or open, flat-bottomed barge, large enough to carry a horse and carriage, until such time as a swing bridge could be constructed. This was pulled back and forth between the two islands by ropes and a hand-operated winch. It was generally known as the 'Horse Ferry' and the berths can still be seen beside the present Watford Bridge. However, it was not until the hurricane of 1887, when the whole of Ireland Island was cut off from the rest of Bermuda for several days by the ferocity of the weather, that it was at last decided to proceed with the proposed structure; but many years were to pass before work commenced.

Watford Island Bridge itself was more than just another bridge. It was the final bridge required to complete the joining of Bermuda's east end to the west end, an event which had long been anticipated as being the major step forward in the development of the Islands as one community.

The contract for the bridge was signed by Messrs. C. H. Walker and Co. Ltd., the same firm which was constructing the South Yard, in 1900, and work commenced in August 1901. The estimated cost was £5,800, towards which the Colonial Government donated £3,800, the Admiralty and the War Department dividing the remaining cost equally between them.

Work continued uninterrupted until the bridge was ready for the official opening on 24 September 1903. In view of the importance of this structure to the economy of the Island, and in particular to those whose livelihood relied on their employment in the naval base, His Excellency the Governor, Lieutenant General LeGuary Geary, KCB, was invited to officiate at the opening, which was marked by a formal ceremony, including guards paraded by the Royal Navy and the Bermuda Volunteer Rifles, ceremonial arches, and a procession of boats, followed by a programme of music and festivities which went on until 11 p.m.

The bridge was manned by four civilian bridge-keepers, at a total wage of £5:3s:9d per day, with a rent-free house for the head keeper. It was open for pedestrians from sunrise to sunset. Once a year the bridge was closed to all pedestrians and vehicular traffic to prevent the creation of a public right-of-way. It was last thus closed on 23 March 1951, just prior to its being handed over to the Bermuda Government.

Between April and November 1957, the bridge was reconstructed and converted from a swing bridge to a fixed structure, the new bridge being officially opened by the Governor, Lieutenant General Sir John Woodall KCMG, KBE, CB, MC, on 12 February 1958, the ribbon being cut by his younger daughter Marian.

The only other bridges in this area are those which were built over the cut to the Lagoon in 1850, and the causeway at the eastern end of the Lagoon, which was similarly opened to allow the flow of water in the same year.

The Islands in the Great Sound

Several of the islands in the Great Sound formed part of the purchase by the Navy in 1809. These were Ports, Nelly, Hawkins, and Long Islands. The original idea behind the purchase of these, and later other islands was to form an isolation hospital and quarantine area for ships arriving from, particularly, the West Indies, where yellow fever and dysentery were rife.

To this end, a hospital was built on Ports Island in 1834, and was used for many years for isolation purposes. The sheltered anchorages around the Islands were similarly used as quarantine anchorages.

Boer Prisoners

The naval islands were not otherwise used for any specific purpose - in fact they were offered in exchange for the army-owned Boaz and Watford Islands in 1823 by Commissioner Lewis, since the latter were far more strategically placed for use by the Navy, but nothing came of this idea. However, during the Boer War at the turn of the century, when several thousand Boer prisoners-of-war were shipped to Bermuda for custody, it was decided to accommodate them on these islands under the custody of the Army.

The first prisoners arrived in Bermuda on 28 June 1901, after several weeks at sea, not knowing where they had come. They were accommodated mainly under canvas in camps set up on Darrell's, Hawkins, Hinson's, Burt and Ports Islands in the Sound, and on Tucker's and Morgan's Islands off Somerset, which are now joined to form the US Naval Annex. The camps on Ports, Hawkins and Nelly Islands were joined by way of Kappa and Eta rocks with wooden footbridges, to enable the prisoners to walk to work on Long Island, where they were mostly employed in quarries at the eastern end or on keeping the cemetery neat and tidy! The island-locked area of water between Long, Nelly and Ports Islands is known, appropriately, as 'Paradise Lake', though it seems unlikely that the Boers used that name for this lovely stretch of water!

The Bermudians were, on the whole, fairly sympathetic to the prisoners, and there was a certain outcry against the harsh conditions under which they were held. A board of enquiry was set up, which completely exonerated the military authorities, and in fact maintained that the Boers were living under better conditions than many of the free Bermudians!

Their confinement did not last long, the last Boers leaving Bermuda in August 1902. During the year of this confinement, a total of 4,619 prisoners were accommodated in the camps. Most of the Boers were repatriated to South Africa; a few remained in Bermuda to settle, and some, inevitably, are buried in the cemeteries on Long Island. There is a monument there erected to their memory, which was consecrated by the Bishop of Newfoundland and Bermuda, the Rt. Rev. Llewellyn Jones, in 1903.

The islands remained as naval property until 1951, when they were turned over to the Bermuda Government in common with the other naval property. The remains of the camp sites, water catchments and drainage channels, as well as the cemetery, can still clearly be seen.

The Sailors' Home, now known as the Mariners' Club, Hamilton.

7

Naval Recreational Facilities

Early Hostels and Naval Canteens

The first recreational hostel was started under the auspices of Vice Admiral Sir James Hope KCB in 1866, who solicited subscriptions from the officers and men of the Fleet to found a Seamen and Marines' Recreation Room. This combined a bowling alley and coffee and ginger beer bar. No alcohol was permitted. The Recreation Room was located just outside the present south gate of the Dockyard, near Moresby House. This was popular for a while, but eventually business fell off; to help with the finances, a Seamen and Marines' Club was started just outside the main gate of the Dockyard, and this did succeed in making enough money to help out its more ambitious neighbour. However, this club was itself closed from lack of support in 1886.

On 12 April 1880, £600 having been promised, and a site granted by the Admiralty, the foundation stone of the Royal Sailors' Home was laid near Lodge Point by Princes Albert Victor and George (later King George V) sons of the then Prince of Wales, who were at that time serving as cadets on HMS *Bacchante* visiting Bermuda. By the following year, £1700 had been expended on the project, which was nearing completion. However, owing to a shortage of cash the home was not finally opened until 1885.

A bowling alley was built in 1887 for £400, which had been donated from the Ginger Beer Fund, but this was little used, and was later converted into the Petty Officers' Club. Extra dormitories were also added at about this time in a separate building.

Between 1904 and 1912, the Dockyard suffered considerable reductions, and both club and canteen fell on bad times, the Petty Officers' Club being opened only when a ship was in Dockyard, about every 6-8 months. World

War I saw a great increase in prosperity however, and considerable improvements were made to the home and the club during this period. It was about this time, to avoid unnecessary confusion, that the names of the two clubs were changed officially to The Royal Naval Canteen and The Petty Officers' Club respectively.

For the officers, there were no facilities until 1 May 1883, when the Officers' Club was opened on a site just to the north of the Cut Bridge. This club was also financed in part by the proceeds from the Ginger Beer Factory, and was expanded to include a bowling alley, and nearby a squash court, during the mid-1930s.

In 1961, the officer complement did not permit the economic running of the club any longer, and it was turned over to NAAFI as the Fleet Canteen.

NAAFI Canteens

It was during World War I that the Navy, Army and Airforce Institute, or more correctly, the Naval Canteen Service, which in 1921 amalgamated with NAAFI, took over the running of the naval canteens in Bermuda. By 1937, NAAFI had built its own handsome building at No. 1 Lane Hill, at the eastern end of Hamilton Harbour. The Fleet Canteen, as the Sailors' Home on Ireland Island South was called, was also handed over to NAAFI.

The Fleet Canteen was a fine building, having the Junior Ratings Canteen downstairs, with a large hall on the first floor, where dances could be held for up to 500 people. This was in frequent use by all naval and civilian personnel and their families. The adjacent dormitory building was in continual use by those sailors, who did not fancy the two-mile walk home to their ships at the end of a riotous evening, and who could hire a bed for the night at a very attractive rate.

When the Dockyard closed in 1951, the canteen was running with a full staff of eight personnel. The farewell dance for those leaving the Dockyard on its closing was held on Boxing Night 1950, and sadly was a farewell in more ways than one, since someone must have left a cigarette burning when the club was shut for the night, and by morning, there was nothing left of the building, but a smouldering ruin. Happily there was no loss of life, and since the Dockyard was then on the point of closing, no attempt was made to rebuild the club. The remains were later razed to the ground.

The canteen was moved to the top floor of the Commissioner's House stables in 1951; the main store, which also supplied the Army NAAFI Shop at Prospect until 1957, being located on the ground floor of the Casemates Barracks.

By March 1956, when the Commander-in-Chief finally left Admiralty

House, the Dockyard had been reduced to a 'Forward Operating Base' activity, and the canteen closed, and was relocated at the Parsonage, the staff being reduced to only three by 1958. This had previously been the 'under-19's Club'; however, in view of the few ships visiting Bermuda, it was only required to be opened when a ship came into the Dockyard, being operated by the ship's own canteen manager, who had to buy in the stock, run the canteen, and return the unsold spirits, beer and food to obliging and long-suffering local traders before the ship sailed, often after a stay of only a few days.

This very unsatisfactory situation lasted for some two years, when a full-time manager was sent out to run this club. The Parsonage continued in use until 1961, when the old Officers' Club, then unused, was turned into the Ratings' Canteen, again with the full-time manager. This could be justified by the increased number of personnel at HMS *Malabar*, and also the larger number of warships of other nations which constantly visited Bermuda for rest and recreation, and for fuelling. Later, the withdrawal of the Navy from its bases in the East also increased the number of ships going west, most of which called at Bermuda at some time during their voyage.

The club soon became known by the sailors as 'The Trap', as it managed to ensnare many who had intended to go further afield for their 'run-ashore', but to whom the lure of duty-free liquor was too great an attraction!

Between 1961 and 1965, there was a very considerable canteen activity, mainly owing to the large number of Canadian ships visiting Bermuda with their base ship, HMCS *Cape Scott*, spending a considerable period alongside. Eventually, from 1962-65, the Canadian Forces opened a canteen of their own at Gilbert's Green.

From 1966, the usage of the club declined. It was opened only when ships were alongside in Ireland Island, or on special occasions for HMS *Malabar* ship's company activities. In the Trap there was a limited families shop facility, and a souvenir boutique was also established on the dockside for the benefit of visiting ships, where curios, post cards etc., were available to sailors, thus saving them the long trip over to Hamilton. In 1970, a club for the families of those serving at HMS *Malabar* was formed, called the 'Star of India' after the crest of HMS *Malabar*, using the old officers' bowling alley as a venue. The need for this club was realised since the families, particularly those living in the married quarters, had nowhere to get together of an evening, since the 'Trap' was only opened when a ship was in the Dockyard, and then it was full of thirsty sailors, hardly a suitable place for families and their children!

During the subsequent two years, the Star developed into a very flourishing and popular addition to the facilities, being run by a committee of the ship's company, with the furniture and drink being supplied through NAAFI, and the ingenuity of the sailors.

Sport

In August, 1872, Captain Moresby, later to be appointed the Captain-in-Charge, who was a very keen cricket player, introduced the game at a carnival held in Somerset to celebrate '40 Years since the unjust thraldom of Slavery'. From this beginning, cricket became the major sport in Bermuda, with the Somerset Cricket Club remaining the undisputed champions for many a year. Unfortunately, they have recently found it more difficult to wrest the crown from their rivals at St. George. The August Cup Match holiday is one of the most popular events in the Bermuda calender.

In order to cater for the recreational needs of the visiting ships' companies, two first rate pitches for rugby and soccer were made on Moresby Plain, which was ideally suited for this purpose, the excavations there having ensured that the area is flat and on a firm rock base. In addition to these pitches, the Royal Navy owned the rugby pitch on Boaz Island, as well as the cricket pitch in Somerset, which is still known as the Royal Naval Field.

For the lesser sports, there were originally four, and later six ratings' tennis courts constructed on Moresby Plain, and a further two officers' courts were laid out near the Lagoon. These were very much used in their day, but there are now just three courts on Moresby Plain. The squash court just behind the old Officers' Club is still in great demand.

Shooting has never been considered much of a sport in the Navy, but there was a pistol range in the Keep Yard, and a full size, one mile long range, situated along the west shore of the Island, for use with the old Lee Enfield rifles, the butts for which are still in being, though very dilapidated. These were, of course, normally used for official practice, rather than for recreation.

Water polo is a sport no longer played in Bermuda, but one which has always been popular in the Navy. Although there were no swimming pools in the Island suitable for this, an area was laid out in between the gangways of the floating dock and many a ship's company fought out a hard game there. At least there could be no cheating by touching the bottom, the water is thirty feet deep at that point!

The Moresby Plain facilities are still available to the Navy, but are currently under-employed, except during visits by more than one ship at a time. Those pitches outside the present Dockyard area were included in the land sold to the Bermuda Government in 1965.

Moresby Plain, showing HMS Malabar *VII, and the large playing field area. In the background can be seen the large Glacis or water catchment, and the casemated land defences of Dockyard, with Commissioner's House in the far distance. Tanks in the foreground (right) are for fresh water storage. The rifle-range butts can be seen in the background at left.* (Official RN photo)

Hospitality Ashore

Bermudians have always been renowned for their hospitality, and friendly attitude, particularly towards the Royal Navy. During World War I, canteens were set up in Somerset by the Imperial Order of the Daughters of the Empire (IODE), which was first founded in Bermuda in March 1911, for the sailors, using War Department and Navy-owned buildings. These operated in addition to the Navy-run clubs and canteens. The IODE was extremely active throughout the war, running voluntary canteen services, providing comforts and organizing dances and socials for the sailors. There is nothing a sailor likes more than getting away from his naval surroundings, and these canteens, with their friendly atmosphere, were very popular and well frequented.

In January 1927, a Sailors' Home was opened in St. George's by Mr. L.N. "Dickie" Tucker. This was moved to new premises on Front Street, Hamilton in 1930, where it remained throughout World War II. In 1947, The Bermuda Sailors' Home, Inc. purchased part of the Imperial Hotel on Church Street. Donations toward the purchase were given in memory of the sailors who had lost their lives in the war. The Home was, of course, open to all mariners, not only those of the Royal Navy, and was the forerunner of the present Sailors' Home on Richmond Road, now called the Mariner's Club, which was opened in 1963 as a result of private contributions and Government support.

At the outbreak of World War II, the IODE once again set up a canteen service, but they had great difficulty in finding appropriate accommodation, since all the suitable naval property was in use. Eventually, they were granted the use of the old Armoury at Mangrove Bay, by the Governor, on 3 June 1940, and this became a most popular and well-frequented place, being open from 10 a.m. to 10 p.m. daily, serving bacon, eggs and chips, coffee and tea, as well as offering friendly conversation to those far from home. The Recreation Hut was used as a billiard room, and Blue Flag, a nearby house, and The Old Post Office building were also used as canteens and dance halls.

Regular dances were held each week, ladies travelling from far and near by train or bicycle to attend. An examination of the accounts makes very interesting reading, with typical entries such as:

Train fares for ladies	5s 0d
Carriage hire	8s 0d
Ingredients for cake	10s 0d
Caretaker, for polishing floor	3s 0d

An average profit, which was of course ploughed back into the funds, was about £20 per evening! This gives a good idea of the popularity of these functions.

Another project undertaken by the ladies of the IODE was the knitting of woollen stockings and comforters for use by the sailors employed on convoy work on the North Atlantic routes. Many letters were received from HM ships at sea expressing the appreciation of the ship's company for these essential aids to comfortable living in arctic waters.

On 30 April 1940, the Ladies Hospitality Organization was founded to formally coordinate the various groups working to entertain the sailors from ships on station and their allies, as they called at Bermuda. The Bermudiana Hotel staff quarters, located on what has become Bermudiana Road, were placed at the disposal of the LHO. The organization was headed by the wife of the Commander-in-Chief and several local ladies, who were assisted by some 500 members who ran the Naval Recreation Club for light meals, afternoon tea and evening entertainment, mainly dancing, throughout the war years. This Ladies Hospitality Organization is the direct forerunner of the present Ladies Guild of the Sailors' Home, which still carries out the same duties, though on a much reduced scale, in view of the smaller number of ships calling at Bermuda.

After the bulk of the Royal Navy Personnel left Bermuda at the end of the hostilities, the clientele of the club was so much reduced that in 1953 the House of Assembly was asked to increase its subsidy from £500 to £1000. However, this was not passed and the club continues to be supported from private subscriptions, and subsidies from the Admiralty and private shipping firms.

Navy Days

The aim of a Navy Day is to introduce the Royal Navy to the people, show them what the service has to offer, and at the same time raise money for naval and local charities. In common with naval dockyards throughout the world, for many years a Navy Day, or Sailors' Home Day as it was called in Bermuda, since all the proceeds went to the Sailors' Home, was held annually.

Several ships and submarines were normally open to visitors, while all around the Dockyard attractions, such as commando and PT demonstrations, handicraft and hornpipe displays, pleasure trips, water polo matches, and cinema shows, as well as the usual fairground stalls, restaurants and side-shows, were all represented. The whole day was usually rounded off with a display of marching and Beating Retreat by a Royal Marine Band.

The last Sailors' Home Day was held on 22 June 1950 - a very sad occasion for many. HM Ships *Glasgow*, *Snipe* and *Sparrow*, together with the Boom Defence Vessel *Barbecue* were alongside and open to the public, as was *Floating Dock No. 5*, and many of the Dockyard workshops. This was the last time that the Commissioner's House was open to the public.

However, there has more recently been a revival in the form of a mini Navy Day when HMS *Ashanti* was undergoing maintenance in November 1973. Many of the old attractions, on a reduced scale, with the addition of a helicopter display, were set up in the South Yard, and were enjoyed by some 3,000 people! The thrills even included a war dance by 'Ashanti Warriors' in tribal costume!

The Ginger Beer Factory

No history of the Dockyard would be complete without mention of this establishment. It is not certain when this enterprise was started, but it was run as a subsidiary to the Officers' Club, as what would now be called a 'Non-public Fund' for many years. However, since it was definitely established prior to there having been an Officers' Club, it must have originally been started by private enterprise. It was manned by a permanent staff of two civilians, and was situated just behind the old Officers' Club premises.

It was, without doubt, a roaring success, paying large sums of money into such worthy causes as:

1872	£102 for founding the theatre in the Old Smithery. Also a sum for the purchase of a billiard table for the Ratings' Club
1882	£640 for erection of the Officers' Club
1889	£600 for reading room and library for Officers' Club; later on a verandah, southern wing and bowling alley were also added.

Many other similar projects also benefitted from the sales of ginger beer, and other soft drinks, and the sight of the horse and cart, or in later years, the Ford motor truck, one of only two in the Island at that time, delivering the minerals around the Dockyard was a familiar one.

The factory continued producing minerals, and paying money to various similar welfare projects until new and stricter hygiene laws coupled with the reduction of personnel serving in the Dockyard, forced the factory to close down in 1944.

8

HMS *Malabar*

The Naming of Royal Navy Establishments

Before embarking on the history of HMS *Malabar*, there is one factor, unique to the Royal Navy and those navies developed under the same system, which requires explanation. Owing to the wording of the Naval Discipline Act, it is necessary for all members of the Royal Navy to be borne on the books of one of Her Majesty's ships in order that the Act should apply to them.

For this reason, with the establishment of the many naval training schools, air stations and other shore establishments and bases throughout the world, each was given a ship's name and commissioned at a formal ceremony, in the same way as a floating ship. Such establishments have become known, for obvious reasons, as 'Stone Frigates'. This unusual practice accounts for the confusion caused to the German propaganda machine during World War II, mentioned in Chapter 1.

It has always been the practice, however, to have a 'Name-Vessel' afloat attached to each such establishment, just to maintain the illusion, and to confuse the uninitiated! The Name-Vessel of HMS *Malabar* was the liberty-boat which plied to and from Hamilton when ships were in Dockyard.

HMS *Malabar* - The History of the Name

Unfortunately, no pictures are known to exist of the first three ships of this name. The following information has been gleaned from the archives at the National Maritime Museum and other sources.

The first *Malabar* was purchased in 1794, having previously operated as the East Indiaman *Royal Charlotte.* She was a fourth rate of 54 guns, tonnage 1,252, and measuring 161'x 42' x 17'6". On 15 April 1796, Vice Admiral Sir John Laforey, Commander-in-Chief on the Leeward Islands Station, detached the *Malabar* under Captain Thomas Parr, with a 64-gun ship-of-the-line, and a few frigates, transports and some troops under Major General John Whyte. On 23 April, this expedition took possession of the Dutch settlements of Demarara and Essequibo, and on 2 May, of Berbice. At Demarara, the *Thetis,* 24, *Zeemeeuw,* 2, and several richly laden merchantmen were taken as prizes. On 10 October 1796, still under Captain Parr, the *Malabar* foundered on passage from the West Indies.

The second *Malabar,* originally named *Cuvera,* was built in Calcutta in 1798 and purchased for £19,719 on 30 May 1804. She was a fourth rate of 56 guns, 935 tons, and measured 168'6" x 37'2". In 1805, she was in use as a store ship with twenty guns. On 2 January 1806, Under Captain Robert Hall, together with the sloop *Wolfe,* 18, she chased two French privateers into the Cuban harbour of Aserraderos. The *Wolfe,* with the boats of the *Malabar,* worked her way into the port and brought off one of the two, the *Napoleon,* 4; the other sinking from the numerous hits she had suffered. On 7 March 1815, the *Malabar* was renamed *Coromandel.* In 1819, she was fitted out to carry convicts to New South Wales and, in 1827, she was again fitted out to receive convicts and lie at Bermuda. In 1853, she was broken up at Bermuda; this being completed in December of that year. A reminder of her days on the Australia run is that the name of the ex-convict colony area of Sydney is Malabar to this day.

The third *Malabar* was a sloop of 20 guns, employed in the Indian Service in about 1810. Unfortunately there is no further information available in the National Maritime Museum Archives concerning this ship, nor does her name appear in the Navy Lists of that time. It is possible that the name was one given by a local Indian authority, without realising that the name was already committed to another man-of-war employed on the other side of the globe at that time.

The fourth *Malabar* was built in Bombay Dockyard of teak at a cost of £56,385, and was launched on 28 December 1818. She was a third rate of 74 guns, 1,715 tons, measuring 174'6" x 48' x 20'. In 1831-32, she was in service off the Tagus. From October 1843, she was in use as a coal hulk, and is recorded in the 1872 Navy List at the coal depot at Portsmouth. On 30 October 1883, she was renamed *Myrtle* and continued in harbour service at Portsmouth. She was finally sold at Portsmouth on 11 July 1905.

By a strange twist of fate, the fourth *Malabar* did visit Bermuda for a week or so in 1838, and so met her predecessor the now-*Coromandĕl,* though probably no one was aware of the coincidence. This *Malabar* had joined the

HMS Malabar *IV leaving harbour. From engraving at Moresby House*

North American Station early in the year and had proceeded to Quebec City with the opening of the St. Lawrence River to spring navigation. As the senior British officer there, her captain, Edward Harvey, received Lord Elgin, when he arrived on HMS *Hastings* on 27 May to take up his appointment as Governor General. This being the summer after the Rebellions of 1837 in Upper and Lower Canada, the *Malabar* remained at Quebec for the summer to act in aid of the civil power, if required.

Fearing a second rebellion after the freeze-up in 1838, Lord Elgin made a request to the Royal Navy in October to move the 93rd Highland Regiment from Halifax to Quebec. Because of the lateness of the season, it was decided that the troops would march to Pictou, N.S. on the Gulf of St. Lawrence to reduce the time of transit. The original plan had not included the *Malabar*, but the necessity of using the frigate HMS *Inconstant* to transport Lord Elgin to England led to her being substituted.

On the morning of 19 October, the *Malabar* was sailing down the eastern shore of Prince Edward Island, with two coasting pilots on board, heading for Pictou harbour. Because of the wind direction, the pilots refused to enter the harbour; instead, it was decided to round Cape Bear on the southeast corner of Prince Edward Island and find an anchorage in Northumberland Strait, where the troops could be embarked. However in the course of doing so, the *Malabar* struck the Cape Bear reef and remained fast.

In spite of firing guns throughout the day, and rockets as well during the night, only one person, Joseph Wightman of Three Rivers, came to offer assistance, and stayed on board until the ship was freed the next morning. Before this was effected, nine upper deck and twenty-seven lower deck guns, together with some shot and anchors, were heaved overboard. The ship had suffered considerable damage and was making three inches of water an hour when able to make her way into Three Harbours to avoid a rising gale. She managed to sail to Halifax, where she was made sufficiently seaworthy to return to England via Bermuda for repairs. Thus *Malabar*(IV) spent a few days in the same waters as *Malabar*(III) (*Coromandel*).

As a postscript to this event, the ship's officers presented Joseph Wightman with a silver service, which was inscribed:

Presented to
Mr. Joseph Wightman
by
Captain Edward Harvey
and the Officers of HMS Malabar
for the important assistance he
rendered to that Ship when
in danger upon the rocks off
Cape Bear
Prince Edward's Island
19 October 1838

The fifth *Malabar* was an Indian Army Trooper, built by Napiers, on the Clyde, and launched in 1867*. She was one of five such ships, run by the Admiralty on behalf of the India Office. Naval Service in these Troopers was not popular as it was regarded as a back-water to promotion. *Malabar* outlasted her class mates, and eventually it was decided to send her to Jamaica to replace the Base Ship there, but a change of orders resulted in the ship being send to Bermuda in 1897. On arrival she was found to be in excellent shape, and became the accommodation ship, being used by the ships' companies of other ships whilst their vessels were in dock.The ship was sold to Messrs. Pearman, Watlington for disposal in 1919, and sailed under tow to the United States for breaking up in February, 1920.

---

* It is of interest that this ship brought to England seven mammoth cases containing 176,602 Suez Canal shares, valued at £3,976,582 which were purchased by Prime Minister Disraeli from the Khedive of Egypt, Abdul Said.

HM Troopship Malabar, *1866-1919, while trooping, pre-1896.*
(Source unknown)

HMS Malabar *V at Portsmouth just prior to her transfer to Bermuda.*
(Source unknown)

HMS Malabar *VI (Commissioner's House) 1919-1951.*
From engraving at Moresby House.

HMS Malabar *VII, Moresby House.* (Official RN photo)

The sixth *Malabar*, built between 1823 and 1827, was originally the proud residence of the Commissioner of the Dockyard. The last such Commissioner, Commodore Sir Thomas Ussher, was resident from 1832 to 1837. At various times after that, the building afforded accommodation for the Superintendent of Convicts, and when the Convict Establishment closed down in 1864, the accommodation was used to advantage by the Artillery and Engineer Officers engaged upon the fortification schemes for the defence of the Dockyard. Some time later, it became a Royal Marines Barracks, and it was not until after World War I, in 1919, that the building finally surrendered its title of Commissioner's House to become HMS *Malabar*, a title it held until finally 'paid-off' on 31 March 1951.

The present *Malabar* is the seventh to carry the name. The house, known as Moresby House, was built in 1899 as the residence of the Officer-in-Charge, Works, an Admiralty civilian officer, whose province was the maintenance and erection of buildings, bridges and roads. It was completely destroyed by a hurricane in 1916, and was rebuilt to its present design at a cost of £9,000 during that year. On the closing of the Dockyard in 1951, the name HMS *Malabar* lapsed for several years.

During the period from 1951 - 1962, the shore offices of the Senior Naval Officer West Indies (SNOWI), a commodore, were established in a small building at the southeast corner of the old Victualling Yard. SNOWI was at first a Sub-Area Commander under the Commander-in-Chief, America and West Indies Station, whose command existed until 1956, when SNOWI became responsible for that area, reporting to the Commander-in-Chief, Home Fleet, in England.

Since the new appointment of SNOWI was essentially a sea-going command, on 15 March 1951, the first Resident Naval Officer, Bermuda (RNO), a Commander of the Supply and Secretariat Specialization, was appointed. He took up residence at The Cottage, carrying out the duties of maintaining a naval presence in the Island, and taking responsibility for all Navy property remaining in Bermuda. His office was in the house in Dockyard Terrace previously occupied by the Foreman Victualler, immediately to the west of the entrance to the Victualling Yard.

In order once more to provide a proper shore headquarters for SNOWI and a base facility in Bermuda, on 1 June 1965, HMS *Malabar* was recommissioned and established in Moresby House, under the command of the then Resident Naval Officer, the building being enlarged to accommodate a communication centre and to house the staff of SNOWI.

In December 1967, owing to a reduction in the naval personnel strength, the appointment of RNO was downgraded, the duties being taken on by the Commodore's Secretary, and at the same time, SNOWI himself took over command of HMS *Malabar*, in addition to his stationwide commitments.

This arrangement proved unsatisfactory for various reasons, the main difficulty being the frequent absence from the Island of SNOWI, and thus the commanding officer of HMS *Malabar*.

It was therefore decided once more that the responsibilities of Commanding Officer, HMS *Malabar* and Resident Naval Officer, Bermuda, could best be undertaken by one person, and that this appointment should be held by a Lieutenant Commander of the Supply Specialization. This decision was fully implemented in March 1971, by the appointment of the author to this post.

The Story of the Indian Trooping Service, 1866 - 1896

Although not strictly within the terms of reference of this book, the following background is of considerable interest in so far as it affects HMS *Malabar* V.

In 1858, it was recommended that a regular service of government transport should be inaugurated. The cost was bound to be heavy, but after much discussion, it was decided to carry the scheme into effect. The Navy was instructed to build and operate five specially designed troopships for the Indian Government.

These ships were built in 1866, but in anticipation of the Suez Canal being opened three years later, they were given dimensions which would permit them to pass through that waterway. They were the *Crocodile, Euphrates, Jumna, Malabar* and *Serapis*, magnificent-looking, rigged (i.e.with masts and sails), screw-driven transports, with a speed of fifteen knots. Each was designed to carry a full battalion with its supernumeraries, about 1,200 men in all. The Indian Government was to pay the bills, but the Navy was to run the ships.

For many years, these ships maintained the routine Indian Trooping Service. In their early days, they were better than anything else on the run, cutting down the passage by a big margin, but as they grew older, they dropped far behind the standards of the contemporary merchantmen and were bitterly criticised. When the P & O liners, which ran along the same route, and generally passed them at sea without any difficulty, were offering excellent comfort and ventilation, the troopers were stuffy and ill-lit.

They were also unpopular with the Navy, for the average officer regarded an appointment to one of the 'Lobster-pots', as they were known, presumably as one 'boiled' when going down the Red Sea, as being a sure sidetrack from promotion. The Admiralty complained that about 1,200 trained officers and men were being used. The India Office retaliated by saying that the Admiralty was charging far too much for its services, and that the money which was supposed to be spent on refits and maintenance in Portsmouth Dockyard was generally spent on some man-of-war whose condition the Admiralty dared not mention to Parliament! No doubt both assertions were based on facts!

As the transports were there and the arrangements were definitely in being, they had to remain in service. They were used for nearly thirty years for the regular Indian relief, although any sizeable campaign forced the Government to turn to the merchant service. Numerous liners were used as troopers in the Ashanti War of 1873, the Zulu War of 1879, the Egyptian Campaigns of the early 80s, the First Boer War, and the Russian scare of 1885.

In the year 1894, the great change was made. The *Serapis* and her sister ships were obviously wearing out rapidly and, with so much money being spent on naval construction, it was doubtful whether Parliament would supply the funds to build ships to replace them. The trooping service was a nuisance to Portsmouth, but the London and South Western Railway was willing to offer superior facilities in Southampton Docks. The *Crocodile, Euphrates, Serapis* and *Jumna* were in such a bad state that they would require a considerable outlay, if they were to continue in service.

So the decision was taken; only the *Malabar* was retained in place of the other four, the *Britannia* and the *Rome* (P & O) and *Dilwara* (B.I.) were taken on charter. The last of the government troopers, the *Malabar*, was discarded before the 1896 season, and shortly afterwards took up her duties as accommodation ship at Bermuda.

A fine contemporary painting circa 1857, by Le Marchant, of the hulk Dromedary, *which was sent to Bermuda in 1826 and was the second hulk used to accommodate convicts working on the Dockyard defences. The hulk is shown alongside the Short Arm of the North Yard. In the background is the Victualling Hulk* Royal Oak. (Reproduced by kind permission of Mr. Jay Bluck)

9

Hulks

There were two types of hulks employed at Bermuda: those which accommodated the convicts, and those which were used by the Royal Navy for the purpose of containing stores, or for accommodation of personnel whose own ships were undergoing refit, etc.

It was a common thing for aged men-of-war to be hulked for these purposes, thus extending their useful life. Basically, all forms of weapons, and gear used solely for sailing the vessels, such as masts, ballast, steering gear, etc., were removed, the belowdecks area fitted out for the required task, and a planked roof built over the upper deck to keep weather out.

The Convict Colony

No dissertation on the Dockyard would be complete without a brief mention of the convict colony, since without the convicts the Dockyard would never have been built in the first instance.

In 1799, the Hulk *Somerset* arrived in St. George's, and moored at what is still called Convict Bay. The convicts she carried were the first to be transported to Bermuda to serve their sentences. They were not, in fact, used on navy works, but the scheme was proved workable, and when, in 1823, the construction of the naval dockyard was proving too great for the locally available work force, further hulks were sent out to provide the labour necessary to undertake the main brunt of the work.

Although employed by the Royal Navy, the convicts were under the control of the Commissioner of Convicts. At first, a Superintendent was sent out from England, but from 1 January 1847, this duty devolved directly on the Governor, by virtue of his office. However, overall control was still maintained by the Superintendent of Convicts in England who appointed convict officers to control the prisoners on a day-to-day basis.

It is quite certain that not all convicts were the irreconcilable rogues we are led to believe. For instance, one draft of convicts was coming to Bermuda in the *Sir George Arthur*, when she ran on the rocks off the North Shore. The captain panicked, the crew mutinied, and it was not until the prisoners were released and took the situation in hand that the ship was saved and sailed into Bermuda.

Among the convicts were many skilled men: architects, engineers etc., who had been convicted of petty fraud or theft and sentenced to up to six years in the hulks. The navy was not slow to make use of their skills, and the help they gave was sometimes rewarded by the remission of sentence.

The arrival of the convicts gave the desired boost to the building of the Dockyard. They built the Commissioner's House, The Cottage and the Parsonage. Those lent to the Royal Engineers built the fortifications, the breakwater and the North Wall. Despite a lull in construction between 1837 and 1848, the work of the convicts ensured that these vast projects were completed by 1863. After 1861, no further convicts were sent to Bermuda

The conditions under which the convicts were held were appalling. They were crowded into old frigate hulls, with temperatures of over 90°F, and 100% humidity. There were few water tanks, and most of the water in them was brackish. It is small wonder that about one quarter of them died. However, one authority quotes them as 'well fed and not overworked'. He seems to find them an unjustified expense to the Public Purse. However, at 3d per day - of which 2d was repaid for food and accommodation charged, it appears that the Dockyard did not cost much in wages.

In 1848, overcrowding in the hulks was so bad that the Crown was obliged to purchase Boaz and Watford Islands from the Royal Navy, and the convicts were at once set to work building a barracks for themselves. These were completed in 1851, and 600 convicts were transferred there from the hulks. The conditions on board in the interim are best left to the imagination. The hulks remained in use for those not fortunate enough to be moved ashore.

Although conditions in the barracks were better and healthier than in the hulks, between 1848 and 1853 more than 400 died of consumption and dysentery. During the forty-year period 1823-1861, 9,094 convicts served in Bermuda, 2,041 of whom died from ailments contracted as a direct result of their conditions of service. Many died of the recurring epidemics of yellow fever. It is of interest that slaves employed under contract from their owners, until emancipation in 1834, on the same work did so unfettered, while many convicts had to work shackled by ball and chain. However, provision was made for their cleanliness in the form of bath-houses - small towers constructed on the water's edge, where the convicts could be locked in while they washed - under strict supervision, of course. One of these remains opposite Little Watford Bridge and another can be seen on the island near Lefroy House.

In 1861, all convicts remaining in Bermuda were housed ashore in the barracks on Boaz Island. These buildings were transferred to the War Department in 1863 when the last of the convicts were returned to England. It was not until August 1930, after many years of haggling, that Boaz and Watford Islands were handed back to the Navy in a very dilapidated condition, the buildings having been virtually unmaintained for many years.

Only one convict was permitted to take his discharge in Bermuda, a Mr. Facey, who later operated a livery stable. On the other hand, a number of the wardens remained in Bermuda, the descendants of several being among prominent Bermudians today.

Convict Hulks

Antelope(58)*	Arrived at Bermuda, bringing the first 300 convicts to work Dockyard. Housed prisoners until broken up in 1844.
Dromedary(20)	Arrived Bermuda 1826. Housed prisoners until at least 1848. In 1863, she was used as a buffer between ships and the Long Arm, as ships-of-the-line could not get alongside owing to the slope of the footings. In that year, HMS *Hero* 'coaled-ship' by cutting a passage through *Dromedary* to give easy access to the jetty, taking on 560 tons of coal in three and a half days, as opposed to the normal 320 tons in a week! This is the last mention of *Dromedary*, which presumably ended her days being used as a fender.
Coromandel(56)	Ex-HMS *Malabar*. Arrived in Bermuda 1827, having previously been used on the Australia run for carrying convicts to the colony since 1819. Broken-up at the Dockyard in 1853.
Tenedos(46)	Arrived in Bermuda 1843. Used for housing convicts until 1848, when she was turned into a convict hospital hulk and moved near to Boaz Island, taking on the convicts who had, between 1823 and that time, been treated at the RN Hospital. She was broken up in 1863, when the last convicts were sent home from Bermuda.

* Figures in brackets show, where known, the number of guns the hulk originally carried, to give an idea of the size.

Thames (46) Arrived in Bermuda 1844. Was first moored at St. George's where there was an outbreak of yellow fever on board in 1853. She was moved to Boaz Island to accommodate those working on the convict barracks, but never lost the taint of yellow fever. It was said that to be sent to her, as convict or warden, was to be condemned to death. She sank at her moorings, unlamented, in 1863.

Navy Hulks

Tourterelle First mentioned in St. George's where she was in service in 1806 as the receiving (or accommodation) ship. In 1810, Commodore Superintendent Andrew Evans hoisted his broad pennant on board, having moved her to Ireland Island to act as the nucleus of the new base. She was relieved almost immediately by the hulk *Ruby*, and was then moored off Hawkins Island as a receiving and hospital hulk, until she was sunk in 1812 to act as a breakwater to give shelter to ships berthed at Ireland Cove, before any construction had begun of the main arms of the breakwater.

Romulus This hulk was moored off Spanish Point and took over the duties formerly assumed by *Tourterelle*. She was used as a ratings' hospital from 1814-18, after which the hulk was scrapped.

Ruby This was one of the first hulks to be employed as a store ship, firstly at St. George's where she briefly took over from *Tourterelle*, and later during the early construction of the Dockyard. She was broken up in 1821, and her timbers were used to delineate the boundaries of the naval property, up until then marked only by a row of yuccas, to 'keep the workmen from wandering', though where they could wander to is a matter for conjecture!

Royal Oak Arrived in Bermuda by 1825. It was proposed that the commodore should hoist his broad pennant on board her, but approval for this did not come in time. In 1834, Sir Thomas Ussher, the last Commissioner, hoisted his broad pennant on board. However by 1842, she had been converted into a victualling hulk, and remained as such until the completion of the Victualling Yard in 1853.

Weymouth Arrived in Bermuda 1828. Used as a victualling hulk and Dockyard storeship from 1832. Transferred to St. George's

A previously unpublished view of the Dockyard in the 1840s by an unknown artist, showing the old Storehouse with its single tower, the completed Great Wharf with the Royal Oak *Victualling Hulk alongside, and the* Dromedary *Convict Hulk at the Short Arm. The hulks at the breakwater are (left to right)* Coromandel, *and* Tenedos. *Note the Camber, and the temporary storehouse where the Victualling Yard now stands, with Commissioner's House at the extreme right.* (National Maritime Museum)

Harbour in 1853 in connection with dredging work.

Medway Arrived in Bermuda in 1848. Used for many purposes. In 1861, a battalion of Marines returning from Mexico was billetted on board.

10

Other Royal Navy Ships Connected with Bermuda

It would take an entire book to list all of the ships which have been based at Ireland Island during its long history, but the following are a few which have some special significance, either from their own point of view, such as the *Shah*, or from episodes in which they were involved at Bermuda, such as *Northampton* and *Warrior*. Although properly a hulk, the *Irresistible* has been included in this section since, although brought out as a hulk from England, she left a greater mark on the Dockyard than her fellow hulks. The *Valerian* disaster, however, has been covered in greater detail in a separate chapter, since this tragedy has not previously been fully published.

Ships Which Served at Bermuda

HMS Irresistible(60)
This was the third ship of the name. She was 2,642 tons, and had a single-screw steam engine, developing some 400 horsepower. The screw was used solely to facilitate movements in and out of harbour. She was one of the last 'wooden walls' of the Royal Navy, her short active life being abruptly terminated as a direct result of the historic engagement between the *Monitor* and the *Merrimac*, during the American Civil War, which so influenced naval construction that the *Irresistible*, built in 1860, was as a 'modern fighting unit', immediately made obsolescent.

Her last appearance in full naval trappings was at Spithead in 1867, when she formed the unarmed division of the Fleet on the occasion of the visit of the Sultan of Turkey to Britain. In 1868, she was hulked at Portsmouth preparatory to her role as accommodation ship at Bermuda. In September of the same year, she was escorted across the Atlantic by HM Ships *Espoir*

HMS Irresistible *alongside the North Arm.* (Source unknown)

and *Viper*, the latter a 'modern' ram, being sent out as part of the Inshore Defence Squadron at Bermuda.

In 1875, the *Irresistible* was used to assist in the erection of the sheerlegs in Dockyard. It was not long after this that a hurricane caused her to heel so badly that she was pronounced as unstable, and large cannon, each weighing some eight tons, which had been awaiting installation in the shore battery, but which had in the meantime become obselete, were placed in her as ballast, presumably with the aid of the sheerlegs which she had helped to install!

After many and continual complaints about her condition and the very poor accommodation facilities onboard, *Irresistible* was placed on the disposal list and sold out of the service in 1891. She was bought by Pearman, Watlington & Co., and moored off Marshall's Island, where she remained until she sank, being finally disposed of by the use of explosives. The four cannon still rest on the bottom where she sank, and can still be seen, though to lift and restore them would be a very costly and difficult manoeuvre.

Her fine figurehead, the only one remaining in Bermuda today, was removed and installed at Clarence Cove, below the old Admiralty House, where it remained until 28 March 1974, when, with the aid of a Wessex 5 Helicopter from RFA *Resource*, it was removed to HMS *Malabar* for custody and later renovation at the Bermuda Maritime Museum.

HMS Shah(26)

The *Shah*, launched at Portsmouth Dockyard in 1873, had been tentatively named *Blonde*, but the official visit of the Shah of Persia to England in 1873 included a visit to Portsmouth and, although gentlemen are said to prefer blondes, the name *Shah* was given to her in honour of the occasion. In return, the Shah, Nasreddin Qajar, who was the first Persian Ruler to visit a European country, gave a commemorative plaque to the ship depicting his name.

The vessel, built of iron cased in wood, with a single screw and with two funnels, was an unarmoured frigate of 6,250 tons, with a 7,000 horsepower engine, and armed with twenty-six guns of various calibre. Her other vital statistics were: length 330 feet, beam 52 feet, and draught 26 feet. She had a complement of 600 officers and men.

After her official trials, *Shah* relieved *Repulse* as the flagship of the Pacific Station in 1876. She was the fastest battleship of her time. In 1877, with a revolution underway in Peru, the maritime situation was somewhat disturbed by the behaviour of the Peruvian turret ship *Huascar*. This single-turretted monitor of 1,130 tons had been seized by the insurgents, and several incidents involving British merchant ships had occurred.

HMS Shah *under steam (left), showing her beautifully sculptured stern and the plaque given by the Shah of Persia, Nasreddin Qajar in whose honour she was named (see detail above).*

The action between Shah *and* Huascar *off Ilo, Peru, 1877. (Source unknown)*

Action between the *Shah* and the *Huascar* took place close to Ilo; there was no loss of life in *Shah* and the casualties aboard the *Huascar* were trifling. *Shah*, by reason of her length, had very little room to manoeuvre with safety and advantage, whereas her smaller adversary employed the shallows and her smaller turning circle to avoid punishment. Although the action was inconclusive, *Huascar* made off, and a little later ceased to be a nuisance in those waters.

While homeward bound in 1879, *Shah* called at St. Helena, Here she received news of the disaster at Islandhlwana, and, taking troops onboard, she sailed for Durban. From the *Shah* and other ships in the area, a naval contingent was assembled, and thus *Shah* could boast not only a private naval action, but a brisk participation in the final stages of the Zulu war. On termination of her active service days, *Shah* was ordered to Bermuda to provide accommodation for naval personnel. When these duties were taken over by HMS *Malabar* V in 1897, *Shah* became a coal hulk, and was moored off Ferry Point on St. George's Island.

In 1900, Admiral Sir Frederick George Denham Bedford, KCB, was appointed as Commander-in-Chief. He had been in command of the *Shah* when the action with the *Huascar* took place, and must have been most grieved to see his former ship condemned to so inglorious an end!

The most unusual sternplaque given by the Shah of Persia is now held in the St. George's Historical Society Museum. It was restored to its original condition by HMS *Malabar* in 1974.

HMS Northampton

On 26 November 1883, the *Northampton*, 7,323 tons, the flagship of the Commander-in-Chief, Vice Admiral Sir John Commerell, VC. KCB, was anchored in Grassy Bay. During the hurricane which suddenly blew up, she broke from her moorings and ran on to the Stagg Rocks.

In order to reduce topweight and refloat her, all her topmasts were lowered, and she was surrounded by a fleet of small boats and lighters, all charged with removing some 600 tons of heavy gear from her to lighten her sufficiently to be towed off the reef.

Owing to the gale, the water within the reef area of Bermuda had built up some four feet higher than usual at the time of the stranding and it was not until HMS *Canada* was sent to her assistance that she was refloated and towed in to the Dockyard on 3 December, where she was repaired.

It is said that the Commander-in-Chief did not leave the bridge of his flagship throughout the time she was aground! It must have added somewhat to his embarrassment when the yacht *Sunbeam*, the private yacht of Lord Brassey, then Civil Lord of the Admiralty, arrived in Bermuda, having weathered the same hurricane a few miles to the south of the Island during a round-the-world cruise with his family!

HMS Scorpion

Launched in 1864 by Lairds of Liverpool, *Scorpion* was one of two such coast defence monitors originally built for the Confederate Navy. Captain James D. Bullock, uncle to the first President Roosevelt, stood by when the ships, under the pseudonyms of *El Tousson* and *El Mounassir*, were building.

Adams, the Federal representative, blocked all attempts at their delivery to the Confederate Navy. The British Government was told that such a step would be regarded as an act of war. An attempt by a French finance business (Bravay Bros.), who said that these ships would be sold, or were intended for the Khedive, was also frustrated by Adams, who also told the French Government that any move by Bravay Bros. would be deemed an act of war. Thus these two ships stayed put and, under the names of *Scorpion* and *Wyvern*, were eventually taken over by the Royal Navy. They cost some £94,000 each. At this time, these two ships were the most formidable vessels afloat.

Scorpion was sent to Bermuda as part of the Inshore Defence Squadron in September, 1869. With HMS *Terror*, and the 'modern' rams *Vixen* and *Viper*, *Scorpion* formed the Inshore Squadron which was deemed necessary to supplement the static fortification system.

In 1901, *Scorpion* became target ship for the flagship, HMS *Crescent*, off St. Catherine's Point. She took the punishment well, and was eventually towed back to Lodge Point, Ireland Island, where she became partly submerged. Eventually she was plugged, and was sold out of the Service to an American firm in 1903. While on tow to Halifax to be broken up, she foundered in a storm off the Massachusetts coast.

HMS Terror

Built at Newcastle in 1856, too late for the Crimean War, or for service in the Northern Theatre/Baltic, *Terror* saw some active service in the Sheerness area before being sent to Bermuda in 1857. Of 1945 tons and 200 horsepower, she was one of four such vessels, the others being the *Etna*, *Glatton* and *Thunderbird*. She was armed with sixteen 68-pdr. guns.

Terror became the flagship of the Captain-in-Charge and was employed in this role until 1903, when she was sent for scrapping and her name given to the *Malabar*, then the receiving ship, and so perpetuated until 1919, when the *Malabar* was in turn scrapped. The name *Terror* was shortly afterwards given to the Naval Base in Singapore.

Terror was the home of the first shore radio installation in Bermuda,

HMS Scorpion, *companion guardship to the sister-ships* Viper *and* Vixen. *The latter was sunk in Chub Cut off Daniel's Head as a block ship.* (Source unknown)

Above: HMS Terror *at her anchorage off the Cottage, with other men-of-war and hulks at anchor beyond in Grassy Bay.* (Source unknown)

Left: One of the blue Minton tiles from the main hatchway of Terror, *depicting Aesop's fable "The Dog and his Shadow"* (Godsiff)

and could transmit eighty miles to ships at sea. After the effectiveness of radio had been proved and accepted, these duties were taken over by the shore facility, then at Daniel's Head.

Some idea of the ornate work, which was still being included in ships-of-the-line of that era, can be gauged from the photograph of one of many tiles which were used to decorate the hatchways of the *Terror*. These were made by Minton, one of the leading porcelain firms in the world.

HMS Warrior

Britain's first ironclad warship, with twenty-two and a half inches of steel plating, covered with teak planking, and displacing 9,210 tons, was HMS *Warrior*. Her claim to fame in the story of Bermuda is that she was one of the ships involved in towing the floating dock *Bermuda* fromMadeira in 1869.

The hull of this fine vessel had since 1929 been in use as an oil fuelling jetty at Pembroke Dock, until being restored and moved to Portsmouth.

The present HMS *Warrior* is the ship-name of the headquarters of the Commander-in-Chief, Fleet at Northwood.

Some of the Ships Built in Bermuda for the Royal Navy

HMS Pickle

After a long period of neglect in the shipbuilding industry of Bermuda, in 1827, three warships were built of cedar: *Pickle* , *Pincher* and *Skipjack*, each of 135 tons displacement. The *Minx* was also constructed on the same lines, but her displacement was only fifty-four tons. She proved to be an extremely fast sailer.

One evening in 1829, the *Pickle* sighted a strange vessel heading for Cuba and gave chase. *Pickle* was a topsail schooner, with a crew of thirty-nine, armed with one 18-pdr and two 8-pdr carronades. The wind was light, but by wetting her sails *Pickle* managed to make use of every breath, and overhauled the stranger. She fired a warning shot and then went alongside. What happened next is best described in the words of her commanding officer, Lieutenant Taflen:

'We reserved fire till we were close on her larboard (port) quarter. The scene was now splendid beyond description. The moon had set and a light breeze was blowing. We could just distinguish the figure of the long, low, black vessel we were engaging as she moved around us, except when by the occasional blazes from her sides on the discharge of her guns, she was distinctly visible. The action continued within pistol shot for an hour and twenty minutes, at the end of which we had the satisfaction of seeing the slaver's mainmast fall'

The captured slaver, the *Boladora*, was found to be armed with sixteen guns and a crew of sixty-two, so *Pickle* had been both outgunned and outmanned. There were 350 slaves in the *Boladora*'s hold. These were released, the crew being put in irons on the slave-deck until the two vessels put in to Havana.

Thus Bermuda can be seen to have played a very real part in the suppression of the slave trade, though of course 350 slaves saved from the plantations was a mere drop in the ocean compared with the tens of thousands shipped across from Africa each year, in spite of the so-called abolition then in being!

Unfortunately, Lieutenant Taflen was drowned in December 1831. He lies buried in the Naval Cemetary.

HMS Firefly

In 1827, Lieutenant Edward Holland designed the *Firefly*, and stood by her while she was being built of cedar by a Mr. Elias Eveson in Devonshire Parish, North Shore. The vessel incorporated Holland's patented sliding keel and is said to have been a very fine sailer.

During the building, Lieutenant Holland lived at Firefly Cottage, North Shore and, on completion, he was, happily, appointed in command of this schooner, surely a unique honour to serve as commanding officer of the ship one has designed and helped to build!

Unfortunately, Lieutenant Holland was invalided to England shortly after assuming command, his place being taken by Lieutenant John Julius M'Connell in 1830.

In 1835, *Firefly* was wrecked off the Honduran coast with the loss of several lives. The ship's clerk, convinced that his commanding officer would not survive, persuaded the survivors to make for Belize, where a search party was organized to look for Lieutenant M'Connell. Some days later, much to the surprise of the clerk, he was found alive!

At the subsequent court martial, which inevitably follows the loss of one of HM ships , the commanding officer and crew were acquitted for the loss of the schooner; however, the clerk was reprimanded for his conduct.

Other Bermuda Built RN Vessels

Bermuda-built cedar vessels were famous throughout the eighteenth century for their speed and durability, and it is not surprising that the Royal Navy had a number of vessels built to their specifications in Bermuda. The following list gives an idea of the number of vessels built for the Royal Navy in Bermuda during the period 1797 - 1809. It is interesting to note the short life of most of these vessels

Name	Date Built	Remarks
CUTTERS		
Alban	1806	Captured in 1810. Re-captured in 1811. Lost off Aldboro's Head in 1812
Barbara	1806	Captured in 1807. Re-captured in 1808. Sold in 1815
Bacchus	1806	Lost in 1807
Cassandra	1806	Lost in 1807
Claudia		Lost in 1809
Laura		Captured in 1812
Olympia	1806	Captured and re-captured. Sold in 1815
Sylvia		Sold in 1816
SLOOPS		
Atlante		Lost in 1813
Bermuda	1806	Lost in 1808
Dasher	1797	Built by Goodrich & Co.
Driver	1797	Built by Goodrich & Co.
Hunter		Contracted for by Captain Pender. Lost in 1797
Indian		
Martin	1809	
Morgiana	1811	
Rover		Contracted for by Captain Pender
Sylph	1812	Lost in 1813
SCHOONERS		
Adonis	1806	Sold in 1814
Alphea	1806	Lost in 1813
Bramble	1809	Sold in 1815
Fierce	1797	Was the *Desperate:* purchased in 1804
Gracieuse		Taken in 1804 from the French
Holly	1809	Lost in 1814
Juniper	1809	Sold in 1814
Mistletoe	1809	
Shamrock		Lost in 1808
Thistle		Lost in 1811
Vesta		Sold in 1816

GUN-SCHOONERS		
Ballahou		Captured 1814
Bream	1807	
Chub	1807	Lost in 1808
Capelin		Lost in 1808
Cuttle	1807	
Grouper		Lost in 1811
Haddock		Captured in 1809
Herring		Sank at Halifax
Mackerel		Sold in 1815
Mullet		Sold in 1814
Pike		Captured in 1807. Re-captured in 1808 Foundered in August 1809
Pilchard		Sold in 1814
Porgy		Lost in 1810
Snapper		Captured in 1811
Tang		Lost in 1808
Whiting		Captured in 1812

Extracts from an Old Diary Kept by Mr L.S.Godsiff

Mr. Godsiff was the clerk to the officer-of-works during the early part of this century. These extracts indicate the most interesting miscellany of vessels which passed through the Dockyard at that time:

1909	18 January	Dutch Warship *Jacob Van Heemskeek* arrived from West Indies. Went into drydock; came out 21 Jan and started coaling a few hours later. Sailed for Holland 22 January at 3.00 p.m.
	11 May	Dutch Warship *Du Rut* left Dockyard
	14 May	HMS *Malabar* went into drydock; came out 24 May
1910	15 January	RMSP *Magdelena* arrived Dockyard; left 16 January with troops
	18 January	SS *Braemar Castle* arrived Dockyard from South Africa; left 20 January with troops
	24 January	German Warship SMS *Victoria Louise* arrived; left for Germany 5 February

	12 February	French Fleet arrived; left 16 February
	7 June	HMS *Shah* went into Drydock
	22 August	German Warship SMS *Fraya* arrived Dock yard; left for South Africa Saturday 27th August
1911	30 January	German Warship *Hansa* left
	20 October	Chinese Warship *Himcs Hai Chi* , commanded by Rear Adm. Ching, arrived Grassy Bay
	21 November	The Fleet arrived Dockyard. HMS *Leviathan* (Flagship) *Berwick, Donegal* and *Essex* in company
1912	16 January	Troopship *Sudan* arrived with troops for Bermuda: left with troops for South Africa 16 January
	18 January	SS *Montrose* arrived Dockyard with 2nd. Battalion Queen's Regiment onboard; left with troops 18 January
	29 January	German Cruiser SMS *Hansa* and *Hertha* left after celebrating the German Emperor's birthday on 27 Jan.
	7 October	French Warship *Descertes* arrived
1913	11 April	HMS *Cumberland* , Cadet Training Ship, arrived from West Indies, Prince Albert among the Cadets. Cadets went to camp at Whale Bay on 16 April, returned from camp 27 April

Other ships mentioned in the diary from 13 August 1908 - 1913, include: HM Ships *Scylla, Cornwall, Brilliant, Indefatigable, Terror, Melpomene, Shah, Aeolus, Rubert*, Surveying Yacht *Ellinor, Alert*, Admiralty Yacht *Collingbine*; SS *Sicilian* , SS *Oruru* , SS *Dahomie* , SS *Port Kingston*; American Training Ship *Ranger*, US Torpedo Boats *Pauling* and *McCall.*

11

The Tragic Loss of HMS *Valerian*

Not a great deal has been written about the loss of the *Valerian* in a hurricane on 22 October 1926, but a brief account of this tragic episode follows. This account has been produced from signals sent at the time and from stories related by people who were present in Bermuda during this sad event.

The *Valerian* had been sent to the Bahamas to offer assistance in the wake of two hurricanes. Having rendered this aid, she was nearing Bermuda on the return voyage, running low on coal and therefore in light condition, when a fierce hurricane struck the area with very little warning, since all the weather reports up to that time intimated the eye would pass some 300 miles north of the Island. Besides, no hurricane had hit Bermuda in October for over 100 years, a dangerous precedent on which to rely!

At 0830 on 22 October, *Valerian* signalled the Commander-in-Chief that she was five miles southwest of Gibb's Hill Light, and hove-to. This was the last signal received from her.

At about noon, the eye of the hurricane passed over Bermuda; there was a lull at 1215, followed by a flat calm until 1320, when the wind shifted from SSE to WNW and increased in velocity dramatically.

The Flagship, the light cruiser HMS *Calcutta*, Captain A.B. Cunningham, was under maintenance at the Oil Berth on South Wall. With the return of the wind, this time blowing offshore at up to 138 mph (at which stage the anemometer broke!), the position of the *Calcutta* became extremely serious. Even though, during the lull, a total of forty wire hawsers had been put out to the shore, and, luckily one anchor had been dropped, the wind, assisted by the tide, which was some 4-5 feet higher than normal in the Dockyard, caused the wires to snap like string, and the *Calcutta* was blown across the basin, coming to rest against the NE Breakwater in the entrance, all the while

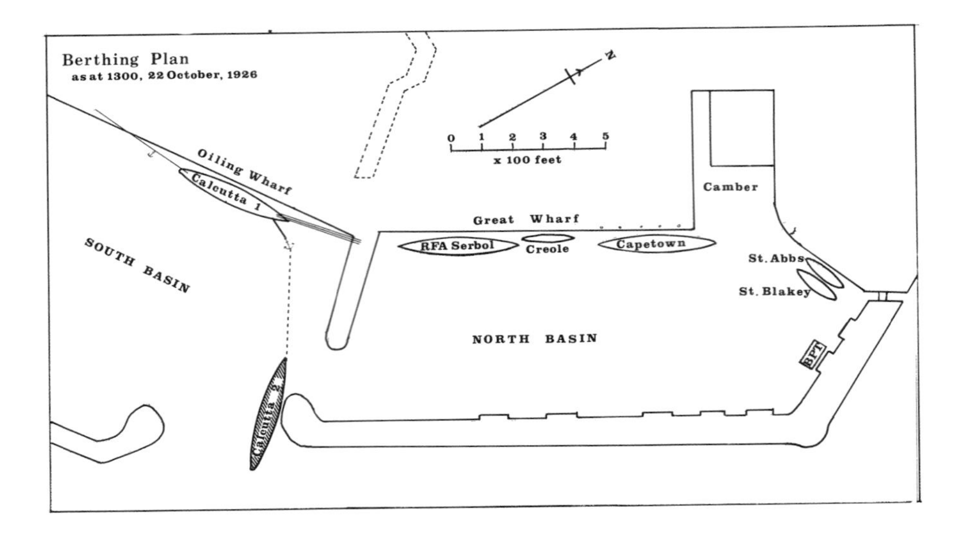

Sketch showing approximate positions of ships and yard-craft in Dockyard at the time of the hurricane. At about 1320 on 22 October, 1926, all but one of Calcutta's *40 wires parted and she swung on her anchor across the entrance, ending up alongside the end of the North Breakwater. Luckily her anchor held, and by using full speed ahead on her engines she managed to maintain her position until the weather abated enough for her to be warped back to the Oiling Wharf at about 1530 with the aid of tugs. At the same time,* Capetown, *in the North Yard, was plunging so much that she drew two of the bollards out of the dockface.*

using full speed ahead on her engines to keep herself head-to-wind! Her radio aerials were blown away early on, which accounts for *Capetown* having to send situation reports on her behalf.

As the ship hit the breakwater, the Executive Officer, Commander H.B. Maltby, and about fifty sailors, leapt ashore and secured the ship with dockyard wires. Two brave sub-lieutenants, Roskill of HMS *Wisteria* (later to become the official Naval Historian of World War II) and Alers-Hankey, of HMS *Capetown*, swam off with lifebuoys attached to grasslines*, and with these two more wires were passed to the shore. This enabled *Calcutta* to reberth at the Oil Wharf when the wind abated. Miraculously, she sustained only superficial damage, all above the waterline.

In the midst of all this, a signalman rushed up to Commander Maltby with a Priority Signal from the Commander-in-Chief 'There will be no tennis at Admiralty House today'!

HMS *Capetown*, in the meantime, was in a more sheltered position in the Inner Harbour, but she was plunging so wildly that she pulled two of the dockyard bollards, to which she was secured, right out of the wharf! Luckily her other wires held, and she ended up reasonably unscathed.

With these problems going on, it is not hard to see how the fate of the *Valerian* came to be overlooked. The next time she was mentioned was at 1610, when the commander-in-chief ordered HMS *Curlew*, another 'C' Class cruiser which had been hove-to off Bermuda throughout the night, to

A Cambrian Class Cruiser leaving the Dockyard. (Godsiff)

* Lightweight, buoyant ropes.

Rescue in the calm aftermath of the hurricane, 23 October, 1926. (Godsiff)

endeavour to get in touch with the *Valerian*. Apparently attempts were made to contact the *Valerian* by radio, but no reply was received. At this time, the *Capetown* reported that she had steam for 20 knots available.At 1757, an urgent SOS from the SS *Eastway* was received, reporting that her bunkers were awash and her hatches broken. The SS *Luciline* at once made towards her, and the SS *Fort St. George* also tried to pick up her position by radio-direction-finder (RDF).

By 1830, the *Eastway* was in dire straits. At 1840, the *Curlew* was ordered to continue the search for *Valerian*. Then with signals crossing each other, she was directed to the *Eastway*, then back to *Valerian* in a matter of minutes. It appears the gravity of the situation surrounding *Valerian* had at last been recognised!

By now darkness had fallen and it was impossible to send extra help from Bermuda, the channel being unlit and impassable at night. *Capetown* was ordered to raise steam to sail at 0600 on 23 October, to continue the search for *Valerian*. *Curlew* continued searching by searchlight throughout the night.

At 0910 on 23 October, *Capetown* reported sighting two men on a raft, and followed this signal with a statement that the men were from *Valerian*, which had capsized and sunk at 1300 the previous day.

The search continued all afternoon and resulted in the recovery of two officers and nineteen men from a total crew of six officers and 103 men. The

A ship of the Pelorus Class alongside the Great Wharf, pre-1930(Godsiff)

Eastway had fared no better - only twelve of her crew were rescued, by the *Luciline*.

Other HM ships in Bermuda weathered the storm well. The *Calcutta* 's damage was minimal, despite the serious position in which she had found herself. *Curlew* sustained upper-deck damage and *Capetown* seems to have come out of it unscathed. No.5 Battle-Practice Target was badly damaged.

The Court Martial, at which Captain Cunningham presided, completely exonerated the survivors of the *Valerian*, and indeed brought out the coolness of these men, and the bravery of Sub-Lieutenant Ronald Summerfield, who lost his life while trying to evacuate men from the engine and boiler rooms. A memorial plaque was set up in the Dockyard Chapel; this was moved to the Methodist Church at Whale Bay, when the Chapel was closed.

As a result of this hurricane, improvements were made to the facilities in the Dockyard, including the resiting of the bollards further from the edge of the dockface, and the provision of special fenders and hawsers for the use of ships caught in harbour during subsequent blows.

Note: Ships and yard-craft in Dockyard at this time were:

HMS *Calcutta*(Flagship)	Oiling Wharf
HMS *Capetown*	Sheerlegs Berth
HMS *Wisteria*	in Floating Dock
RFA *Serbol*	40ft Fenders
St. Abbs(Tug)	Old Coaling Wharf
St Blazey(Tug)	Old Coaling Wharf
Creole(Tug)	Great Wharf(refitting)
No. 5 Battle Practice Target(BPT)	NE Corner
AFD No.1	South Yard(sunk to 3ft above keel-blocks)

Other Navies Based in Bermuda

The Naval Examination Service - 'The Bermudian Navy'

The major role of Bermuda in World Wars I and II was that of a collecting point for transatlantic convoys, supplying urgently required food and munitions to a beleagured Britain. A brief description of the Examination Service appears in Chapter 1, but the following is an account of that service during the 1939-45 War.

In order to control, check and reroute the merchant ships, an examination service was formed, consisting of locally entered reserve officers and men who were based at a building in Convict Bay, St. George's, and whose duty it was to board and inspect the papers of every ship entering Bermuda waters.

The scheme was introduced in May 1939, when a trial run using HM Ships as 'Blockade-runners' was held. This successfully exercised the wits of the examination officers who met with passive resistance, an uncooperative 'Italian' Skipper, and hoards of jabbering 'Italian Maidens' - none of whom could - or would - speak English! To help with the realism it was a foul day, and the Governor, who was in the pilot boat to witness the exercise, left in a hurry, suffering from 'mal-de-mer'!

From 29 August 1940, the service was in operation in earnest. A Furness-Bermuda tender, the *Castle Harbour*, was commandeered and her crew was made responsible for carrying out the requirements of three examination officers, two naval signalmen and eleven pilots. A 14-foot service dinghy was all they had to make their precarious way between the *Castle Harbour* and the ships being inspected. The Chief Examination Officer remained ashore, in comparative luxury, in St. David's Battery!

A fine model of the Gladisfen, *the tug which played such a big part in the directing of convoys during World War I.* (Shadbolt)

The primary duty of the examination vessel was to stop and investigate the papers of all merchant shipping and minor war vessels not equipped with recognition signals. Once vetted, they were given a two-flag clearance signal for the day and were allowed to proceed. In cases of difficulty, the militia at Fort St. Catherine were empowered to open fire; but in fact this never occurred, though there were several occasions where a warning shot was required to encourage a ship to stop for inspection!

The examination officers were not required to carry out a thorough search of any vessel; they had to assure themselves there was no reason to doubt the credentials of any ship. Should there be any doubt, the vessel was ordered to anchor in Murray's Anchorage, under the control of the shore batteries, while a full examination was carried out by a special search party.

The control point for communications - which were of course all done by light, semaphore or flag hoists, since there were no walkie-talkie sets in those days - was the Port War Signal Station (PWSS), at Fort George, certainly the busiest Service Establishment in Bermuda, and the forerunner of the present Harbour Radio. There was, of course, considerable rivalry between those serving in the *Castle Harbour* and the PWSS, since one only had to relax for a few minutes to miss a signal, or not be looking when being 'flashed-up' prior to a message being passed, and thus incur the wrath of the man at the other end!

Weather was a critical factor. The winter of 1939-40 was one long to be remembered by the examination officers - particularly the boarding of HMS *Valiant* on Christmas Day in a strong northerly gale - not really the ideal conditions under which to go out in a 14-foot dinghy!

After the initial period, it was found unnecessary to have two boarding officers and two signalmen, and the team was reduced to one examination officer, and one pilot. This was a far less cumbersome team and became a great deal more efficient as a result. The very bulky 'Examination Officers' Log' was also discontinued - through lack of supply - which caused sighs of relief from the officers, who had trouble enough clambering aboard ships themselves, let alone carrying this vast tome under one arm!

When the *Castle Harbour* was being refitted, a much smaller Furness-Bermuda vessel, the *Bermudian*, was called into service. This was far too small even to serve hot meals, and frustration was the order of the day when, returning from an early Examination for breakfast, another ship hove in sight and the boat had to steam back to Five Fathom Hole with its crew of hungry men still onboard!

Moreover, the bridge was tiny, and when signals were being passed and course was altered there was an ungainly rush from one side to the other in an endeavour to keep the signalman, trailing his Aldis lamp with its twenty feet of wire cable, in sight of the Signal Station!

Although Examinations were normally only carried out in daylight hours, a night patrol was maintained. During the early days of the War, the ex-Mersey ferry, *Woodside* - long since discarded by her original owners - was called back to serve her country. She was unseaworthy, ancient and unreliable, but somehow her crew managed to keep this 'temporary warship' - armed with only two rifles - at sea until early 1940, when she was replaced by the armed yacht *Owera*, herself built in 1907!

In May 1940, Bermuda became a convoy assembly port, and the Naval Control Service was established, which incorporated the Examination Service, to cope with the increased flow of ships. Their old and faithful vessel was commissioned as the HMS *Castle Harbour* on 1 July 1940, and thenceforward flew the white Ensign, being commanded by a Lieutenant in the Royal Naval Reserve. She was also armed with an ancient 3-pounder gun, depth charges, and fitted with ASDIC (now called SONAR) gear, to operate which an officer and four ratings were provided.

From this time on, the role of examination vessel and antisubmarine patrol vessel were combined, and the *Castle Harbour* maintained a continuous patrol throughout daylight hours.

The method of boarding an incoming ship varied with the weather. In rough seas, the dinghy would be launched in the lee of the ship; in fair weather, it could be dropped well ahead and heaved alongside by the crew holding on to the boat-rope lowered for this purpose. It was obviously very undesirable to keep a large tanker wallowing in heavy seas in the very restricted waters, and extremely high degree of seamanship was required at all times to keep delays to the absolute minimum.

When there was a queue of ships to enter, the intrepid men in the dinghy were often towed from one ship to the next by the examination vessel. This was a hazardous, and wet occupation, as 14-foot dinghies are notoriously apt to plough under when being towed, and great care had to be taken to get the examination officer onboard without submerging him in the attempt!

Sailing day for convoys was usually about every fourth day. Outgoing convoys were given priority over vessels entering, which had to heave to off Five Fathom Hole, under the eye of one examination vessel, while the other ferried pilots to and from the ships leaving, as there were seldom enough pilots to go around.

The activity was high until May 1942, when the Bermuda convoys were discontinued. During that summer, two new vessels were added to the 'Fleet' - the *Sumar* and the Norwegian Whaler *Gvas* II. The *Owera* was withdrawn and sent for duty in Jamaica. One day, a submarine scare was received at a time when the *Castle Harbour*'s crew were all ashore. To save face, as senior officer of the group, the Captain put to sea with his first lieutenant on the helm, a couple of deck hands and a galley boy to serve as chief engineer, or mate-of-the upper-deck, as required! Needless to say, no contact was made as no one knew how to work the Asdic! But honour was satisfied, and the Commander-in-Chief never found out the truth!

Early in 1943, HMS *Castle Harbour* was withdrawn for refit and transfer to the Mediterranean, but she was torpedoed and sunk in the Caribbean.

At this time, the American convoys started. These consisted of up to 97 ships in each convoy, all of which had to be fed through the Narrows to the assembly point, then sailed as required for Europe. Once in the anchorage, the US Forces were responsible for the ships, but the volume of vessels transiting gave the Examination Service and the pilots a tremendous task. During this period, there was a continuous flow of landing craft being steamed from the United States to Britain in preparation for the D-Day Landings, and these smaller craft had to be fitted in with the main traffic flow.

In May 1944, the American convoys ceased, but at the same time the US

Naval Operating Base in the Great Sound was building up in importance and the flow of ships to and from the base was almost continuous, taxing the resources of the pilots to the utmost. It was, and still is, the rule that only British warships may enter or leave without a pilot. However, a rule crept in that US Navy ships could dispense with a pilot after transiting twice inwards and once outwards. The number of ships using the Channel during this period was over 1,000.

From early 1944, with a reduction in the convoy traffic, the life of the examination officer became easier, and they were taken out to ships in the pilot boat only when required, instead of spending long hours on station.

On the closing of hostilities in Europe in 1945, the Examination Service was disbanded, having coped in a magnificent manner with over 3,000 ships of all shapes, sizes and nationalities, ranging from dirty, smoky tramps to luxury P & O Liners. A truly magnificent achievement by Bermuda's own 'Navy' - the men of the Examination Service.

Daniel's Head and the Royal Canadian Navy

The area around Daniel's Head in Somerset was purchased by the Royal Navy with the land at Ireland Island in 1809, but was not developed for many years.

With the introduction of wireless telegraphy, this site was used as the Royal Naval W/T Station, a job for which it was ideally suited by reason of its open ground, which was required for the aerials.

The site was in constant use during World War I, but after the war, and with the advent of shortwave radio, the site lost its importance and it was dismantled, the two masts being felled on 15 October 1926.

The area was then partly turned over to a pig farmer, and partly to the youth service, which for many years ran camps there for visitors and local children, using existing buildings and tents for shelter.

On 1 January 1963, the Royal Canadian Navy rented eleven acres of land at Daniel's Head for the purpose of building a radio station. The lease, which was not signed until some two years later, was for twenty-one years from the original date of occupation, at a rent of £2,000 per annum, with certain clauses included to make the beach available for recreational purposes to those serving at HMS *Malabar*.

With the change of title of the Canadian Forces, the base became known as the 'Canadian Forces Station, Daniel's Head', in 1969, and was one of the first Canadian Stations to be manned by the new-look unified Canadian Forces personnel.

On the outbreak of World War II, the Royal Canadian Navy set up a static Antisubmarine School in Casemates Barracks, under the auspices of the Royal Navy. It was not until the Royal Navy gave up its work-up Base in Bermuda, in August 1944, that the Royal Canadian Navy decided to take over this facility, and established a small antisubmarine base at Convict Bay, St. George's, which was commissioned as HMS *Somers Isles*.

This base was used for the working up of ships in an antisubmarine role, a submarine being detached to the area for this purpose. The *Somers Isles* was only in commission for about twelve months, but during that period approximately 125 warships of the Royal Canadian Navy were put through their paces from this small establishment.

Since that time, the Canadian Forces have adopted a different approach to the problem of work ups by establishing a permanent liaison officer in Bermuda, and detaching ships and aircraft from Canada two or three times each year to work up in the very suitable practice areas off the Island, using the facilities of HMS *Malabar* and the US Naval Annex to berth their ships in between exercises. This system works well, and means a regular influx of some six to eight warships for a period of up to three or four weeks on each occasion.

The United States Forces in Bermuda

Although not strictly within the terms of this history, the influence of the United States Forces has been so revolutionary in Bermuda that a brief mention must be made of them.

During World War I, the US Navy opened Naval Base No. 24 on White's Island in Hamilton Harbour, rented for a period of ten years for this purpose, which was operational from March 1918 until January 1919, being used mainly in connection with anti U-Boat and convoy-escorting duties. The lease lapsed when the War ended.

On the outbreak of World War II, the British and Allied Powers decided that it was essential to set up air and naval bases around the world, with the aid of the United States, who, though not at that time combatant, was a friendly nation.

Bermuda was one of the Islands where the United States was given free land concessions, on a 99-year lease, in return for their assistance, and in September 1940, the agreement was signed giving the United States an area around St. David's Island for development as an airfield, and also two islands off the Sandys'-Southampton boundary for a naval operating base.

Construction commenced almost at once and lasted until 1943, by which time the project had cost the United States about $43,000,000 (£17,520,320).

One of the major problems encountered was that of transport. In those days there were no tarmac roads in Bermuda and the transporting of heavy equipment around the Island over dusty roads was obviously most undesirable. In May 1941, a law was passed, with a great deal of opposition, permitting motor cars to use the public highway, but it was not until 1945 that the first paved road, from Kindley Airforce Base to Hamilton, was constructed by the Bermuda Government, and the following year the extension to the Naval Operating Base was built by the United States Government to ensure proper communications between the two bases.

In the meantime, most equipment and stores were transferred by horse-drawn vehicles, or sometimes by the railway, which was not a very efficient means of transport since its nearest point to Kindley was one and a half miles away. The railway, a narrow gauge track, was built in 1931, and ended its days in 1947, being sold to British Guyana.

Another difficulty which beset the project was the bridge across Castle Harbour which allowed access to St. George's. The original causeway, opened in 1871, ran from Blue Hole to St. George's Island via Long Bird Island. The dredging and filling involved in the construction of the airfield necessitated cutting this causeway and rerouting it around the west end of Long Bird Island.

In the early stages, a temporary bridge was installed, made of a lighter, which supported planks to each side of the road. This caused a great deal of trouble with the variation in tide, and even more difficulty during rough weather, when the lighter bucked and twisted as if alive! It was not until some ten years later that the United States authorities constructed a swing bridge, which was first opened for traffic on 4 December 1952. Its first refit was in 1973, after it had been unable to swing for some years, when a temporary Bailey Bridge was put up by the Bermuda Regiment to enable the traffic flow to continue throughout the repairs, which took some months to complete.

The airfield opened officially, though on a very reduced scale, on 29 November 1941. A clause included in the Bases Agreement earlier that year at the instigation of the Bermuda delegates to the London Bases Conference, ensured that 'the airfield would be made available to civilian traffic when the war situation permitted.' Since then, a great many improvements have been made and it is now a fully operational international airport, serving the civilian and military needs of Bermuda.

In 1970, command of the airfield changed from the United States Airforce to the United States Navy, at the same time the Naval Operating Base became an annex to the main command, and was reduced to a small refuelling and accommodation area.

Appendices

Appendix 1

A Pictorial Depiction of Naval Property, 1795-1975

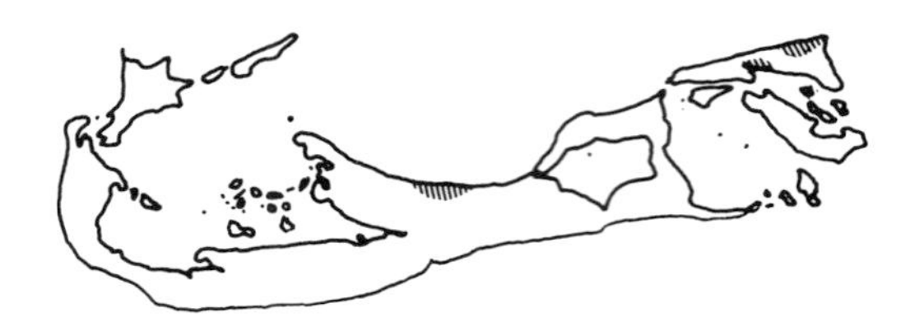

1795-1808
Sites in St. George's at Secretary's Point and Hen Island. Tobacco Bay watering tanks. Naval Wells purchased on North Shore

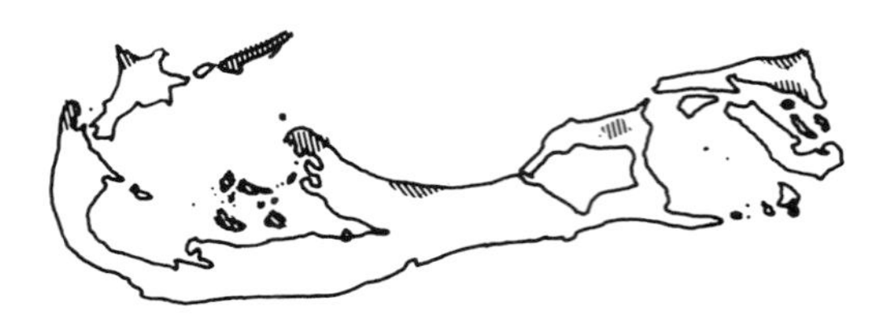

1809-1833
Purchase of Ireland Island and St. John's Hill. Also Wreck Hill and Sound Islands. Mount Wyndham leased (Hamilton Parish) and Spanish Point purchased. Period of initial construction at Dockyard.

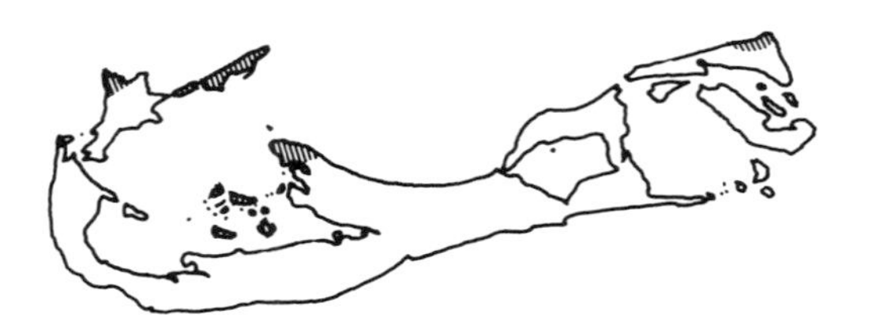

1834-1900
St. George's abandoned as a naval base. Watering tanks retained until 1867. Construction of North Yard completed about 1863, when convicts left Bermuda.

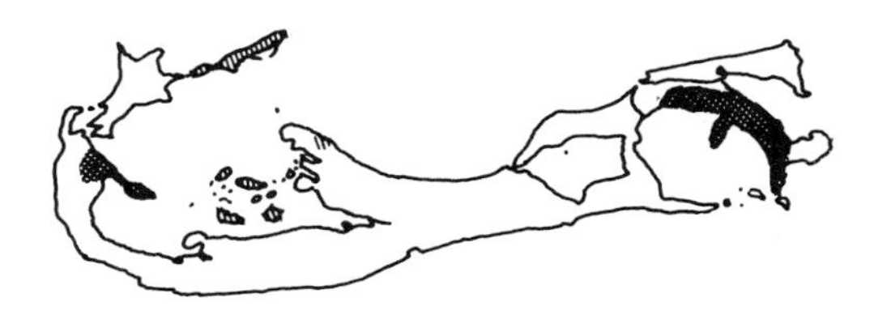

1901-1950

Daniels Head vacated 1926. Economy drive caused half of Dockyard to be closed in 1929. Fully operational during World Wars I and II. US built airfield and Naval Annex in 1941. Great Sound Islands sold gradually in this period.

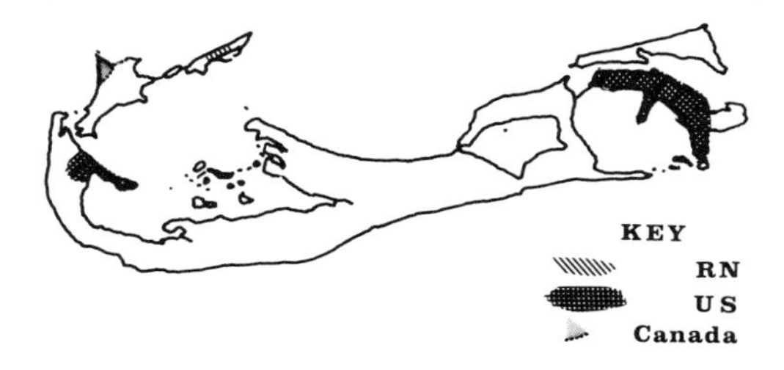

1951-

31 March: Dockyard reduced to skeleton staff and most RN property sold to Bermuda Government. Further rationalisation in 1956. Small portion rented back on 99-year lease. Daniel's Head rented to Canada on 1 January 1963 for 21 years

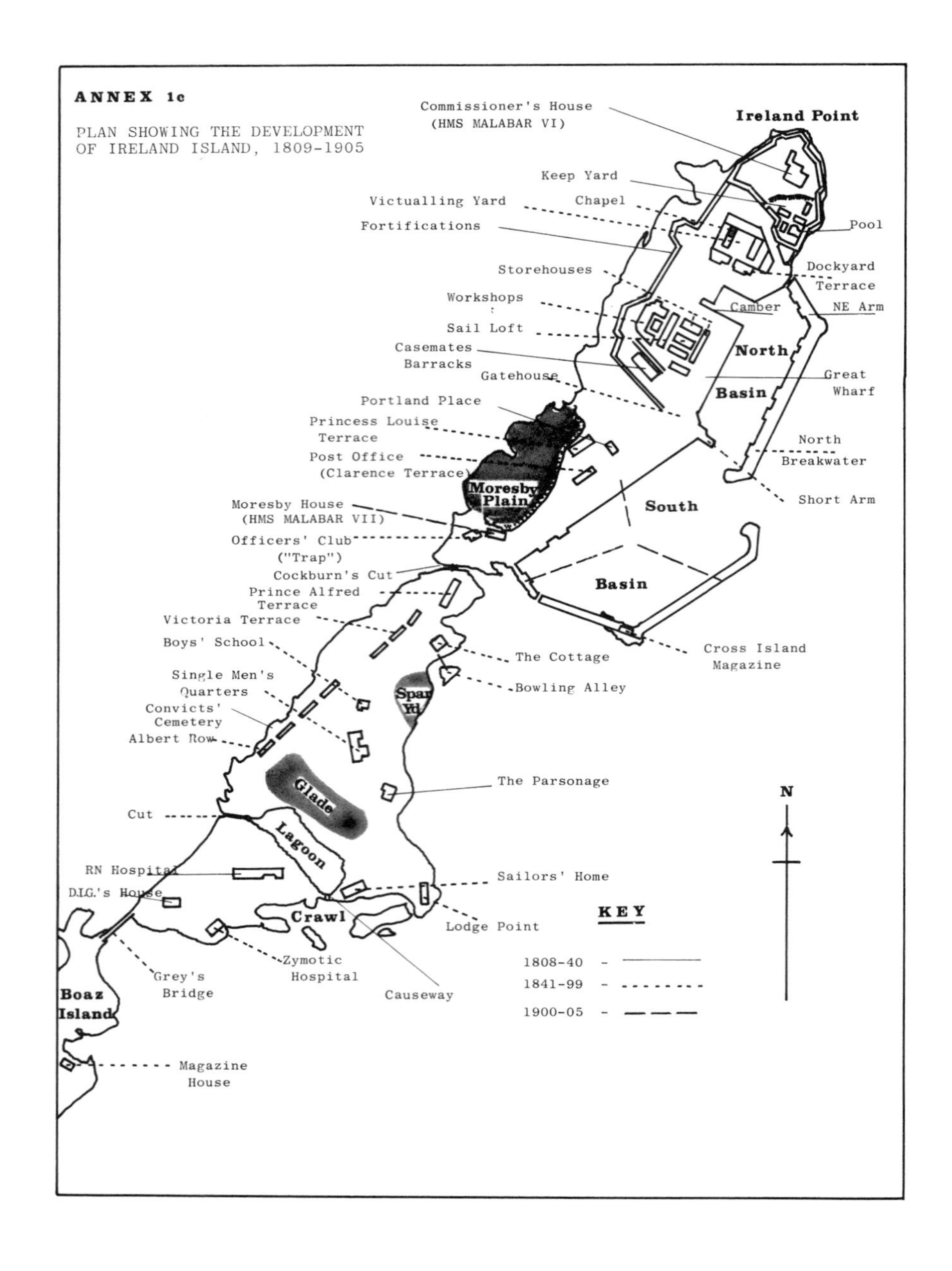
ANNEX 1c
PLAN SHOWING THE DEVELOPMENT OF IRELAND ISLAND, 1809-1905
Commissioner's House (HMS MALABAR VI)
Ireland Point
Keep Yard
Victualling Yard
Chapel
Fortifications
Pool
Storehouses
Dockyard Terrace
Workshops
Camber
NE Arm
Sail Loft
Casemates Barracks
North Basin
Gatehouse
Great Wharf
Portland Place
Princess Louise Terrace
North Breakwater
Post Office (Clarence Terrace)
Moresby Plain
Short Arm
Moresby House (HMS MALABAR VII)
South Basin
Officers' Club ("Trap")
Cockburn's Cut
Prince Alfred Terrace
Victoria Terrace
Boys' School
The Cottage
Cross Island Magazine
Single Men's Quarters
Bowling Alley
Spar Yd
Convicts' Cemetery
Albert Row
The Parsonage
Glade
N
Cut
Lagoon
RN Hospital
Sailors' Home
D.I.G.'s House
Crawl
Lodge Point
KEY
Zymotic Hospital
1808-40
1841-99
1900-05
Grey's Bridge
Causeway
Boaz Island
Magazine House

Appendix 2

Chronological Synopsis of History of the Royal Navy at Bermuda

Note:	Dates for buildings are, as far as can be ascertained, the dates of commencement of construction, unless otherwise stated.

1794	Captain Hurd completed survey of Bermudas (1783-94) HMS *Cleopatra* (Captain Penrose) transited Narrows to Murray's Anchorage Naval Watering Tanks constructed at Tobacco Bay. First used by HMS *Hermione*
1795	Approval for purchase of Ireland Island. Site chosen by Captain Pender Admiralty House at St. George's Naval Wells purchased from Mr. Robinson Wreck Hill purchased with a view to constructing a Light house (never developed beyond foundations)
1795-1809	Cottages built on Hen Island, St. George's. Adaptation of wharf for careening at St. George's
1802-04	St. George's abandoned as a Naval Base, then re-opened with Mr. Dunsier in charge
1806	*Tourterelle* at St. George's as Receiving Ship
1807	Construction of shore fortifications
1809	June 12th. Purchase of Ireland Island. Erection of several wooden wharves, storehouses etc., for supplies for two '74s', 6 Frigates and 2 sloops December. Main Guardhouse built near Spar Yard
1810	Admiral Sir J.B. Warren rented St. John's Hill as the residence for Commander-in-Chief

	Tourterelle moored off Tatem's (Hawkins) Is. as Hospital Ship
	Old Storehouse building (single tower)
1811	First Commodore Superintendent, Andrew Evans, hoisted Broad Pennant in *Tourterelle*
1812	CinC granted Mt.Wyndham (Hamilton Parish) by Legislature; St. John's Hill became a Naval Hospital
	Tourterelle sunk to give shelter to ships in the Camber area
	Naval Cemetery at Ireland Island consecrated
1813	Spanish Point rented by Admiralty for Peppercorn rent
1814	Blacksmith's shop in Spar Yard, RN Hospital, Ireland Island
	Romulus hulk moored off Spanish Point as ratings' hospital
1815	Houses overlooking Grey's Bridge area
1816	Officers' houses on north side of Ireland Island
	Also one for the Commissioner (all demolished 1827)
	Admiralty House given to Navy by Government for Commodore Superintendent at St. George's
1817	Captain John Lewis, first Commissioner, appointed
	Cockburn Cut opened by Royal Engineers (re-filled in 1823)
1818	The Square, Artisans' Houses. (Portland Place)
	RN Hospital opened
1819	Admiralty House surveyed
	Surgeon's house at RN Hospital
	Foremen's houses
1820	Steam Factory, Smithery and Storehouses
1821	Improvements and wine cellars at Admiralty House
	Ruby hulk broken-up; timbers used to delineate Dockyard
1822	St. John's Hill re-named Clarence Hill
	Abbot's Bay became Clarence Cove.
	Further survey of Admiralty House
	4 Horses bought to replace slaves at Dockyard
1823	Clearing and blasting at Dockyard.
	23 UK, 218 local employees in Dockyard
	Cockburn Cut closed
	Commissioner's House commenced October.
	Antelope hulk brought first 300 convicts, plus 20 RM officers, 393 other ranks, and first Naval Chaplain
1824	More convicts arrived
	Casemates commenced
1825	Ropewalk, at northwest side of Maria Hill
	Smithery and saw pit
	Lagoon entrance closed by causeway

	Royal Oak hulk arrived for use as Victualling Hulk
1826	NE Breakwater reached 200 feet, growing at 13 feet per month
	Foundation of SE Breakwater
	Dromedary hulk arrived
1827	The Cottage, the Parsonage.
	Fortifications and Keep
	Great Wharf
	First Commissioner moved in to Commissioner's House
	Convict hulk *Coromandel* (ex-*Malabar* II) arrived in Bermuda
1828	*Weymouth* hulk arrived
1831	Two careening capstans installed on Camber
1832	Admiral Sir E. Griffith-Colpoys (CinC) died.
	Buried in Naval Cemetery (November)
1833	First Steamship-of-War at Bermuda - HMS *Rhadamanthus* - en route Jamaica to London, coaled at Bermuda
1834	Slaves freed 1st August
	Ports Island made into Quarantine Area
	St. George's finally abandoned as a Naval Base
1836	Hurricane breached NE Breakwater; stops work on Timlin's Narrows
1837	Great Wharf finished; NE Elbow finished
	Post of Commissioner abolished; Mr. Ballingall, Naval Store-keeper assumed charge; lived at the Cottage
	Commissioner's House became residence for Superintendent of Convicts
	First buildings in Keep Yard
1838	Interior work begun on NE Arm of Breakwater
	Foundations for Lighthouse at Wreck Hill
	HMS *Malabar* IV visited Bermuda for repairs
1839	Exterior work begun on NE Arm
	Ports Island and RN Hospital improved
1840	Boat Slip at the Camber; Houses near Spar Yard
1841	May. Vice Admiral Sir Thomas Harvey KCB (CinC) died at Clarence House
	Dockyard Main Gatehouse
	Workmen's houses near RN Hospital
1842	Last of original wooden buildings
	Victualling Yard.
	Wall of North Yard
1843	South (short) Arm Completed
	SW Guard House.

	Lodge Point Houses
	Tenedos hulk arrived
	Cockburn Cut re-opened to allow stone-barges through
	Wooden bridge constructed over gap
	18 August. Violent hurricane did great damage to buildings
	Worst yellow fever outbreak - 1047 ill, 114 died
1844	Boy's School
	Thames hulk arrived
1845	Albert Row 1-4
	Plumbers Shop in Spar Yard
1846	Gibb's Hill Lighthouse completed
	Mortuary at RN Hospital, in hut by Lagoon
	Victoria Row 17-24
1847	Albert Row 5-8
	Small Slip for *Pickle* in Spar Yard
	Boat Repair Shed (North Yard)
	Stables and Shed in North Yard
	Breakwater in North Yard Completed
1848	Boaz Island bought for Convict Barracks
	Naval Wells pronounced as 'bad' by Lord Dundonald
	Medway hulk arrived
1849	Rails and trucks providing for coaling
	Smithery
	Magazine in Keep Yard
	Victualling Yard: Dockyard Terrace
	Watford Cemetery opened for convicts
	Grey's Bridge
	More of Victoria Row
1850	Magazine on Sober (Cross) Island
	Boaz Island Barracks completed
	June. Mr. Ballingall ordered to lay out top floor of No. 2 Victualling Store as a Chapel
	Cut at west end of Lagoon opened to allow flow of water
	Large Magazine in Keep Yard
	Grey's Bridge opened
1851	Shipwright's Shop: Cooperage (North Yard)
	The Oratory (ex-slaves' quarters) opened as chapel
	Organ received for Chapel from USA
	Convicts moved into new Quarters on Boaz Island (600)
1852	Foundry and Fitting Shop
	Victualling Yard completed

	Ports Island Isolation buildings
1855	6 houses in Dockyard Terrace completed
1857	Mr. Ballingall retired.
	Captain F. Hutton became first Captain in-Charge and hoisted his Broad Pennant in HMS *Terror* : moved into Cottage
	Naval Storehouse complex.
	Old Storehouse finally demolished.
	East Storehouse (Clock Tower building) completed
1858	More houses at Victoria and Albert Terraces
	Steam Pumping Engine House and chimney
1859	Lodge Point transferred to War Department
	Boat Shed and Engine House in Spar Yard
1860	Sail Loft and Water tank (underneath)
	Gun Mounting Store
	Further 12 Houses at Victoria Terrace and Albert Row
1861	All convicts accommodated on Boaz Island
	East and West Wings added to RN Hospital
1862	Commissioner's House transferred back to Navy.
	112 RMs barracked there
	Total personnel and families on Navy property - 865
1862-67	Seven houses of Prince Alfred Terrace
1863	7 Knuckles installed to enable ships to berth alongside NE Wall.
	All remaining 136 convicts shipped to UK in April
	Start of period of intense activity in Dockyard; 700 men employed
1866-67	Seamen's and RM's Recreation Room opened
	Naval Watering Tanks at Tobacco Bay transferred to Army; use as Naval facility discontinued
	Single Men's Quarters on Maria Hill
1868	Saw Mills
	HMS *Irresistible* arrived as Accomodation Hulk
1869	28 July. Floating Dock *Bermuda* arrived; berthed in Grassy Bay
	HMS *Scorpion* arrived as Floating Battery
1870	Floating Dock moved into Camber
1871	Opening of Causeway
1872	August. Captain Moresby started Sandys Cricket at a Carnival.
	Spar Yard Theatre
	Officers' Billiard Room

1873	Sailors' Home (100 beds)
1875	Constructor's Repair Ship
	Officers' Quarters at RN Hospital
	Sheerlegs set-up
1876	Engine House for Sheerlegs (demolished 1929)
	Officers' Quarters at Ports Island Hospital
	Pitch House on NE Arm
1877	Seamen's and RM's Club near Dockyard Gate
1878	Dispenser's House at RN Hospital
	Cottages near Spar Yard
	Captain-in-Charge's bowling alley
	Post Office and Cottages
	Floating Dock badly damaged in hurricane
1879	St. David's Lighthouse completed
	Princess Louise Terrace (4 houses)
	HMS *Malabar* (V) arrived Bermuda as Accommodation Ship
1880	12 April. Foundation Stone of RN Sailors' Home laid by Princes Albert Victor and George (later George V)
	Captain-in-Charge's Boat Shed in Spar Yard
1881	Girl's School
	Shed on Boat Slip in Camber
	Railway Lines in Dockyard for coaling
1882	Galvanizing Shop
1883	RN Officers' Club. RN Warrant Officers' Club
	Plumbers' Shop. Boiler House
1885	Sailors' Home opened near Lodge Point
1886	Single Men's Quarters
	Seamen's and RM's Club closed (lack of support)
1887	Cable Tanks constructed
1888	Bowling Alley at Sailors' Home
	Torpedo Boat slip at Spar Yard
189-	HMS *Vixen* sunk in Chub Cut off Daniel's Head
1891	Boilmaker's Shop. Coal Sheds (810 tons)
	HMS *Irresistible* scrapped
1892	Cockburn's Cut bridged by a poured-concrete structure
	More coal sheds. Carpenter's shop
	Two-Rock Passage opened
	Duty-free privileges accorded to Navy (but not to Army)
1893	Torpedo Store in Dockyard
	Captain H.J. Carr appointed as Captain-in-Charge. (Wrote the first history of the Dockyard)

1897	HMS *Malabar* V arrived as Receiving Ship
1899	Coal Sheds (4,300 tons) on Victualling Wharf
	Zymotic Hospital. Crawl House (Dentist's residence)
1900	Moresby House (Officer-in-Charge, Works residence)
1901	Contract let to Messrs. Walkers for extension to Dockyard (South Yard) 28 June.
	Boer Prisoners arrived in Bermuda
	Watford (swing) Bridge construction started (August)
1902	New Floating Dock, *AFD No.1*, again largest in world at that time, left Sheerness 16 June. Moored off Boss's Cove onthe day before Coronation Day (8 August 1902)
	August. Boers repatriated
1903	Cemetry on Long Island consecrated
	HMS *Terror* scrapped. Name passed to HMS *Malabar* V which then became the Headquarters Ship
1904	Sailors' Club reduced to 'Ship-visit-only' openings
	Floating Dock *Bermuda* grounded at Spanish Point
1906	6 June. Floating Dock *AFD No. l*, moved from Boss's Cove to Dockyard
1907	Dockyard extensions completed
1911	Enlarging of Town Cut commenced (20 feet depth)
1914	Outbreak of World War I. Canteen re-opened on full scale
1915	3 September. 82 mph hurricane caused considerable damage.
	Yacht *Pearl* (CinC's) smashed
1916	23 September. 84 mph. hurricane caused 'complete wrecking' of Moresby House. Damage cost over £9,000 to repair
	Examination Service established
1917	1 January. Enlarged Town Cut opened (22 feet depth)
	US Naval Base No. 24 established in Bermuda on White's Island.
1919	January. US Naval Base No. 24 closed down
	Dockyard reduced to only 400 personnel
1920	Vice Admiral Sir T B W Napier, KCB,MVO, Flag Officer Commanding 4th and 8th Cruiser Squadrons, died at Admiralty House. Buried in the Glade, 30 July
1922	21 September. 110-120 mph hurricane
1924	Dundonald Channel completed
1926	15 October. Daniel's Head Radio Station closed down
	22 October. Hurricane (over 136 mph) caused Flagship *Calcutta* to break adrift.

	HMS *Valerian* sank off South Shore with the loss of 4 Officers and 84 men
	80-ton crane constructed
1929	Economy drive caused closing-down of half of Dockyard
1930	RN Club, Cottages and Canteen extended.
	Control of Ammunition store in Keep Yard passed to RN
	21 February. Sheerlegs 'struck'
1932	Dockyard Recreation Club. Bowling Alley at RN Officers' Club
	Short-wave Radio Station at Dockyard extended
1933	RAF Station Bermuda established in the Dockyard
1939	Naval Examination Service established
	RAF Station transferred to Fleet Air Arm and moved to Boaz Island
	3 September. Outbreak of World War II
1940	September. US granted land at East End and Great Sound on rent free 99-year lease
	5 November. Armed Merchant Cruiser, HMS *Jervis Bay* fought off German Pocket Battleship *Admiral Scheer* and saved Convoy HX 84.
1941	*AFD. No. 48* arrived Dockyard
1942	July. SS *City of Birmingham*, bringing urgent essential supplies to Bermuda, sunk by U-boat, leaving Bermuda with only 2 days' supply of flour
1944	HMCS *Somers Isles* commissioned at Convict Bay
	April. RN Air Station Bermuda closed down
	Ginger Beer Factory closed down
1945	Naval Examination Service disbanded
	HMCS *Somers Isles* paid-off
1946	*AFD No. 1* returned to UK
	AFD No. 5 arrived Bermuda
1950	22 June. Last 'Sailors' Home Day' held in Dockyard
	Grey's Bridge re-constructed
	26 December. Sailors' Home burned down (unintentional fire)
1951	31 March. HM Dockyard Bermuda closed down
	HMS *Malabar* VI paid-off
	21 December. King's Colour laid-up at St. John's Church
	Surplus RN Property in Bermuda sold to Bermuda Govern ment
	First Resident Naval Officer appointed

	11 July. *AFD No. 5* left for UK under tow of HM Tugs *Warden* and *Reward*
1953	King's Colour (2nd set) laid-up at St. James Church, Somerset
1956	28 October. Queen's Colour laid-up at Bermuda Cathedral
	29 October. Last Commander-in-Chief America & West Indies Station hauled down his Flag.
	First Senior Naval Officer West Indies (SNOWI) hoisted his Broad Pennant
	Remainder of Naval Property sold to Bermuda Government, with the land required for future operations being rented back on a 99-year lease by the Navy
1957	New Watford Bridge constructed
1963	1 January. Canadian Navy leased Daniel's Head on 21-year lease
1965	1 June. HMS *Malabar* VII commissioned at Moresby House
1970	Magazine House, Boaz Island, became Residence of Commanding Officer, HMS *Malabar*
1972	November. RN Hospital razed by (intentional) fire
	AFD No. 48 sunk to west of Ireland Island
1974	24 January. Admiralty House razed by (intentional) fire
1976	1 April. Post of SNOWI abolished

Appendix 3

Officers on Station

A. List of Commanders-in-Chief 1767-1956

Showing the various names for the Area of Command

North America

1767	Commodore Samuel Hood
1770	Commodore James Gambier
1771	Admiral John Montague
1774	Admiral Samuel Graves
1776	Admiral Lord Howe
1779	Admiral the Hon. John Byron
1779	Admiral Marriott Arbuthnot
1780	Admiral Thomas Graves
1781	Admiral Marriott Arbuthnot
1781	Rear Admiral the Hon. Herbert Rigby
1782	Commodore Sir E. Affleck
1783	Commodore Sir Charles Douglas
1785	Rear Admiral Sir Herbert Sawyer
1789	Rear Admiral Sir Richard Hughes

River St. Lawrence and Coast of America and North America and West Indies

1794	Vice Admiral the Hon. G. Murray
1796	Vice Admiral George Vandeput
1800	Vice Admiral Sir W. Parker, Bt.
1802	Vice Admiral Sir A. Mitchell, Bt., KB
1806	Vice Admiral the Hon. J.C. Berkeley

Vice Admiral Sir Andrew Mitchell, KB, Commander-in-Chief 1802-05, who died in office and was buried in St. George's Cemetery. (Source unknown)

1807	Vice Admiral Sir J.B. Warren, Bt., KB
1810	Rear Admiral H. Sawyer
1812	Vice Admiral Sir J.B. Warren, Bt., KB

North America

1813	Vice Admiral the Hon. Sir A. Cochrane, GCB
1814	Rear Admiral Sir Edward Griffiths

North America and Lakes of Canada

1816	Rear Admiral Sir D. Milne, KCB
1818	Rear Admiral Sir Edward Griffiths

North America and Newfoundland

1821	Rear Admiral W.C. Fahie, CB
1824	Rear Admiral W.T. Lake
1827	Rear Admiral Sir Charles Ogle

North America and West Indies

1830	Rear Admiral Sir. E. Griffith-Colpoys, KCB
1832	Vice Admiral the Rt. Hon. Sir G. Cockburn, GCB
1836	Vice Admiral Sir T. Halkett, Bt., KCB
1837	Vice Admiral the Hon. Sir C. Paget, GCB
1839	Vice Admiral Sir Thomas Harvey, KCB
1841	Vice Admiral Sir Charles Adam, KCB
1844	Vice Admiral Sir Francis Austin, KCB
1848	Vice Admiral the Rt. Hon. Earl Dundonald, GCB

Vice Admiral Sir J.B. Warren, KB, Commander-in-Chief 1807-10, who was responsible for the purchase of Ireland Island, 21 October, 1809. (Source unknown)

1851	Vice Admiral Sir G.F. Seymour, GCB
1853	Vice Admiral Arthur Fanshawe, CB
1856	Vice Admiral Sir Houston Steward, KCB
1860	Vice Admiral Sir Alexander Milne, KCB
1864	Vice Admiral Sir James Hope, KCB
1867	Vice Admiral Sir Rodney Mundy, KCB
1869	Vice Admiral George G. Wellesley, CB
1870	Vice Admiral E.G. Fanshawe, CB
1873	Vice Admiral George G. Wellesley, CB
1876	Vice Admiral Sir A. Cooper Key, KCB,FRS
1878	Vice Admiral Sir E.A. Inglefield, CB,FRS
1879	Vice Admiral Sir L.F. M'Clinton, FRS
1882	Vice Admiral Sir John Commerrell, VC,KCB
1885	Vice Admiral the Rt. Hon. Earl Clanwilliam, CB, KCMG
1886	Vice Admiral Sir Algernon Mc. L. Lyons, KCB
1889	Vice Admiral Sir George Willis Watson, KCB
1892	Vice Admiral Sir John O'Hopkins, KCB
1895	Vice Admiral Sir James E. Erskine, KCB
1897	Vice Admiral Sir John Fisher, KCB
1899	Vice Admiral Sir Frederick Bedford, KVB
1901	Vice Admiral Sir Archibald L. Douglas, KCB
1904	Admiral Sir Day H. Bosanquet, KCB
1907	Rear Admiral Frederick S. Inglefield

Fourth and Eighth Cruiser Squadrons

1909	Rear Admiral Arthur M. Farquhar, CVO

Vice Admiral the Rt. Hon. Earl Dundonald, GCB, Commander-in-Chief 1848-51, who ensured the completion of the building of the Dockyard by his energetic and forceful approach to the problems involved. (Source unknown)

1911	Rear Admiral Edward E. Bradford, CVO
1913	Rear Admiral Sir Christopher Cradock, GFM,KCVO,CB
1914	Rear Admiral R.S. Shipps-Hornby, CMG
1915	Vice Admiral Sir George E. Patey, KCMG,KCVO
1916	Admiral Sir Montague E. Browning, GCMG,KCB,MVO
1918	Rear Admiral Sir Morgan Singer, KCVO,CB
1920	Vice Admiral Sir T.B.W. Napier, KCB,MVO
1920	Vice Admiral Sir W.C. Packenham, KCB,KCMG,KCVO
1923	Vice Admiral Sir Michael Culme-Seymour, BT, KCB, MVO

North America and West Indies

1924	Vice Admiral Sir James E. Fergusson, KCB,KCMG
1926	Vice Admiral Sir Walter H. Cowan, Bt, KCB,DSO,MVO
1928	Vice Admiral Sir C.T.M. Fuller, KCB, CMG, DSO
1930	Vice Admiral Sir Vernon H. Haggard, KCB,CMG
1932	Vice Admiral the Hon. R.A.P. Plunkett Ernle Erle Drax, CB, DSO
1934	Admiral the Hon. Sir Matthew Best, KCB, DSO, MVO
1937	Admiral Sir Sidney Meyrick, KCB
1940	Admiral Sir C.E. Kennedy-Purvis, KCB

Western Atlantic

1942	Vice Admiral Sir Alban T.B. Curteis, KCB
1944	Vice Admiral Sir Irvine G. Glennie, KCB

America and West Indies

1945 Vice Admiral Sir Irvine G. Glennie, KCB
1946 Admiral Sir William G. Tennant, KCB,CBE,MVO
1949 Vice Admiral Sir Richard V. Symonds-Taylor, KBE, CB, DSC
1951 Vice Admiral Sir William G. Andrewes, KBE,CB,DSO
1953 Vice Admiral Sir John F. Stevens, KBE,CB
1955 Vice Admiral Sir John W.M. Eaton, KBE,CB,DSO,DSC

B. List of Senior Naval Officers West Indies 1956 - 1975

Senior Naval Officer West Indies

1956 Commodore G.E. Hunt, DSO,DSC
1958 Commodore W.J. Parker, OBE,DSC
1960 Commodore H.C.J. Shand, DSC
1961 Commodore J.E.L. Martin, DSC

Senior Naval Officer, West Indies
and Commander British Forces, Caribbean Area

1962 Commodore J.E.L. Martin, DSC
1963 Commodore E.B. Ashmore, DSC,ADC
1964 Commodore H.H. Dannreuther

Senior Naval Officer, West Indies
and (NATO) Island Commander, Bermuda

1966 Commodore J.M. Townley, ADC
1968 Commodore M.N. Lucey, DSC,ADC
1970 Commodore D.G. Roome, MVO,ADC
1972 Commodore C. Rusby, MVO,ADC
1974 Commodore B.J. Straker, OBE*

Senior British Officer, Bermuda

C. List of Superintendents, Commissioners, and Captains-in-Charge, Bermuda 1795 -1951

Superintendents

1795 Captain T. Pender, Flag Captain and Superintendent, St. George's

*The appointment of Senior Naval Officer West Indies was abolished lst April, 1976

?	Mr. J. van Norden, Storekeeper, St. George's
1804	Mr. W. Dunsier, Secretary to Commander-in-Chief, Storekeeper and Superintendent, St. George's
1811	Captain A. Evans, Commodore Superintendent. Pennant flown in *Tourterelle* hulk at Ireland Island
1817	Captain J. Lewis, Captain Superintendent

Commissioners

1817	Captain J. Lewis
1823	Captain T. Briggs
1829	Captain C. Inglis
1829	Captain J. Ayscough
1832	Captain Sir T. Ussher, KCB

The title of Commissioner was abolished, Sir Thomas Ussher being made Commodore Superintendent in 1832

1837	Mr. S. Ballingall, Storekeeper-in-Charge and Superintendent

The post of Commodore Superintendent was abolished in 1837, the duties being undertaken by Mr. Ballingall until he retired in 1857

Captains-in-Charge

1857	Captain F. Hutton
1863	Captain F.H. Glass, CB
1865	Captain J.F. Wainwright
1868	Captain G. le G Bowyer, CB
1871	Captain E. d'O Aplin
1876	Captain L.E. Somerset
1878	Captain J. Moresby
1881	Captain T. Barnardiston
1884	Captain J.F. Grant
1887	Captain R.P. Denistoun
1889	Captain R.G. Kinahan
1892	Captain H.J. Carr
1894	Captain J.W. Brackenbury, CB, CMG
1896	Captain C.P.G. Hicks
1897	Captain R.P. Humpage (Temporary appointment)
1897	Captain W.H. Piggott
1899	Captain T. McGill

1902	Captain H. Leak
1905	Captain H.H. Bruce
1906	Captain N. Grant
1909	Captain B.H. Fanshawe (Grandson of Capt. Fanshawe RE, who was responsible for the survey and design of the Fortifications at Dockyard in 1826)
1911	Captain G. Corbett
1914	Captain D. Tatton-Brown
1918	Captain F. Morgan-Singer, CB
1919	Captain B.H. Fanshawe
1921	Captain J.F. Grant-Drifon
1922	Captain A.B. Baker, DSO
1922	Captain C.H. Pitcher, DSO
1924	Captain A.T. Tillard, DSO
1926	Captain C.A.M. Sarel, OBE
1928	Captain R.V. Holt
1930	Captain H.B. Maltby
1932	Captain F.H.G. Walker
1934	Captain E.K. Boddam-Whetham, DSO
1936	Captain E.C. Denison, MVO
1938	Captain J. Powell, DSO (later Rear Admiral) - recalled for war service.
1942	Rear Admiral G.W. Taylor (retired) - re-called for war service.
1944	Rear Admiral C.H. Knox-Little (retired) - re-called for war service
1946	Captain S.V. Jephson
1948	Captain J.A. McCoy, DSO
1950	Captain J.T. Lean, DSO (until 28 February, 1951, when appointment of Captain-in-Charge was abolished on the closing of the Dockyard)

D. List of Resident Naval Officers, Bermuda 1951 - 1975

Resident Naval Officer, Bermuda

1951	Commander G.D. Ardron*
1954	Commander L.W.B. Cotching
1956	Commander W.G. Jack
1958	Commander R.T. Owen

* Appointment commenced 15 March, 1951

HMS Malabar*'s Ship's Company, 9th March, 1973* (Official RN Photo)

1960 Commander J.P, Parker
1962 Commander W.J.N. Rutherford
1963 Commander J.G. Brisker

Commanding Officer, HMS *Malabar*, and Resident Naval Officer, Bermuda

1964 Commander J.G. Brisker
1966 Commander A.J. Boyd

Resident Naval Officer, Bermuda

1967 Lieutenant Commander J. Williams (Also Secretary to SNOWI)
1970 Lieutenant Commander R.J. Barcham (Also First Lieutenant, HMS *Malabar*)

Commanding Officer, HMS *Malabar*, and Resident Naval Officer, Bermuda

1970 Lieutenant Commander R.J. Barcham
1971 Lieutenant Commander B.I.D. Stranack
1974 Lieutenant Commander R.A. Godfrey
1976 Commander D.I. Aldrich
1978 Commander T.D. Kitson
1981 Commander T.H. Green

Commanding Officer, HMS *Malabar*, Resident Naval Officer, Bermuda, and NATO Island Commander, Bermuda

1982 Commander T.H. Green
1983 Commander T.E. Woods
1986 Commander J.A. Startin

E. Officers in Charge of Departments, HM Dockyard, Bermuda, 1795-1951

Naval Store Department

Naval Store Keeper and Clerk of Cheque

1795-1803 J. Van Norden
1803-1817 John Dunsier
1817-1830 Thomas Irving
1830-1831 Bernard Ballard
1831-1857 Joseph Ballingall

Naval Storekeeper and Agent Victualler

1857-1866	John Martin

Naval and Victualling Storekeeper and Accountant

1866-1876	Thaddeus Dismont
1876-1880	Andrew Visard
1880-1885	W.A. Mount
1885-1892	H.J. Laslett
1892-1899	H.C. Maule

Naval and Victualling Store Officer and Cashier

1899-1901	W. Smith

Naval and Victualling Store Officer

1901-1903	E.A.S. Hayward
1903-1904	R.J. Hall
1904-1909	C.F. Stivala

Deputy Naval Store Officer

1909-1913	D.S. Griffiths
1913-1917	R.A. Pitcher

Naval Store Officer

1918-1922	F.M. Palmer
1922-1926	W.H.L. Roberts
1926-1929	H.S. Webb
1929-1932	E.H. Codling
1932-1935	W.J. Locke
1935-1937	G.F.R. March
1937-1940	H. Reynolds
1940-1944	F.G.A. Francis
1944-1945	W.F. Cobb
1945-1947	W.C. Beach
1947-1949	H.C. Borner
1949-1951	F.E. Finnemore

HM Victualling Yard

Agent Victualler

1828-1830	H. Ditmas
Sep 1830-Oct 1850	S. Triscott

Naval Storekeeper and Agent Victualler

1850-Apr 1857	J. Ballingall
May 1857-Feb 1866	J. Martin

Victualling Storekeeper and Accountant

Feb. 1866-Oct 1876	T. Dismont

Naval and Victualling Storekeeper and Accountant

Oct 1876-Mar 1880	A. Vizard
Mar 1880-Aug 1885	W.A. Mount
Sept 1885-Dec 1892	H.J. Laslett
Dec. 1892-Jul 1899	H.C. Maule

Naval and Victualling Store Officer and Cashier

Jul 1899-Jul 1900	W. Smith
Jul 1900-Jul 1901	J. Dean

Naval and Victualling Store Officer

Jul 1901-Feb 1903	E.A.S. Hayward
Feb 1903-1904	R.J. Hall
Feb 1904-Oct 1909	G.F. Stivala
Oct 1909-Jan 1913	O.S. Griffiths
Jan 1913-Feb 1917	R.A. Pitcher

Deputy Victualling Store Officer

Feb. 1917-Apr 1920	E.J. Gill
Apr. 1920-Nov 1922	R.C. Beaumont

Assistant Victualling Store Officer

Nov 1922-Dec 1925	T. Hewson

Deputy Victualling Store Officer

Dec 1925-May 1926	T. Hewson
May 1926-Aug 1928	F. Lemarie
Aug. 1928-Apr 1932	S.W. Evans
Apr 1932-Apr 1935	J.R. Ellis
Apr 1935-Mar 1938	T.G. Martin
Mar 1938-Mar 1940	J.G. Marsden
Jan 1940-Oct 1942	A.H. Rook

Senior Temporary Assistant

Oct 1942-Sep 1945	J.N. Ashworth

Deputy Victualling Store Officer

Sep 1945-May 1949	L.J. Coker
May 1949-Apr 1950	J.A. Nicholson
Apr 1950-Mar 1951	E.F. Blyth

Royal Naval Armament Depot

Officer in Charge

1918-1923	Lt.J. Wright R.N.
1923-1928	Comm. Gunner F.C. Worsley R.N.
1928-1930	Comm. Gunner W. Fogg R.N.

Deputy Armament Supply Officer

1930-1934	M. May
1934-1936	W.H. Newman
1936-1939	D. Todd
1939-1945	G.S. Steed
1945-1948	M.M. Little
1948-1950	J.E. Boyce

Sources and Acknowledgements

Books and Newspapers

A Sailor's Odyssey, Viscount Cunningham of Hyndhope
Bermuda from Sail to Steam, 1784-1901, Dr. H.C. Wilkinson
Black Cargoes, Daniel Mannix
Bulwark of Empire - Bermuda's Fortified Naval Base, 1860-1920, Lieutenant Colonel Roger Willock, USMR
Isle of Devils, Sister Jean Kennedy
Voyage of the Sunbeam (1876-77), Lady Brassey
'Bermuda: the Growth of a Naval Base', Paymaster Lieutenant W.E. Brockman RN, *The Royal Gazette*, 5-23 May, 1938
'Naval History of Bermuda from the Earliest Times', Captain H.J. Carr RN (1893), *Bermuda Historical Quarterly* , 1951
'Account of life on the Convict Hulks', William Sydes, alias Jones, one of the Convicts, *Bermuda Historical Quarterly*, 1951.
'The Examination Service', *Bermuda Gazette and Colonist Daily*, 28th May, 1945 et seq.

Museums and Records

Bermuda Archives and Reference Library
Booklet on Boer Prisoners
Notes on US Navy in Bermuda

The British Library
Map of Ireland Island by William Hack, 1694 (Published by permission of the British Library Board. Shelfmark: Add. MS 5415.G.14)

The Ministry of Defence (Navy)
Record of appointments of Officers

Copies of early charts (Hydrographer of the Navy)
Various photographs as acknowledged in the text

The National Maritime Museum, Greenwich, London
Mid 19th Century watercolour of Bermuda showing the harbour with hulks, by an unidentified artist

Photographs and Sketches

Unless otherwise acknowledged, all photographs and sketches have been taken, or drawn, by the Author. Where some photographs and original drawings have come into my hands from unknown original sources, these have been marked 'Source unknown'. Should copyright have thus unwittingly been infringed, it is hoped that this apology will be accepted as acknowledgement in good faith.

In particular, grateful thanks is extended to the following for permission to publish photographs owned or taken by them:

Mr. Brian Shadbolt	(Cover picture, *Gladisfen*)
Mr. H. Godsiff	(Many photographs)
Miss F.K. Stranack	(Admiralty House)

Personal Help

My grateful thanks are due to the following:

Mr. J. Bluck, Heritage Antiques, Bermuda: Original paintings by Sir Gaspard Le Marchant, c. 1857, and permission to reproduce two of these.
The late Mr. Forster Cooper: Maps and plans left after the closing of the Dockyard in 1951.
Sir John Cox, for recollections in connection with the stranding of the Floating Dock *Bermuda*
Lieutenant A.E. Nicoll, RNR, JP, for information about the World War I Examination Service and for lending the model of the tug *Gladisfen*

- and many others for information, photographs and memories, in particular Mr. H. Godsiff, and Mr. E.H. Gladwin, MBE, who have contributed so much by way of personal recollections to this work; and to Sir Gilbert Cooper, Kt, CBE, ED, for his help and encouragement.

General Index

Ship Index